The Anzacs at Gallipoli

Scarecrow Army

The Anzacs at **Gallipoli**

Scarecrow Army

Leon Davidson

First published in 2005 by

black dog books

15 Gertrude Street, Fitzroy Vic 3065, Australia
+61 3 9419 9406
+61 3 9419 1214 (fax)
dog@bdb.com.au
www.bdb.com.au

Designed by Ellie Exarchos
Maps by Guy Holt Design
Printed in China by 1010 Printing International Ltd

Photos credits:
Cover — lower: *Gallipoli Peninsula, Turkey. 1915. Australians and New Zealanders in a
front-line trench at Anzac.* (Australian War Memorial C03420)
Cover — upper: *Soldiers of an unidentified unit of the 2nd Australian Division carrying full
equipment, climbing a steep slope on Gallipoli.* (Australian War Memorial P02905.003)
Page i: *A sniper in the trenches at Pope's Hill.* (Kippenberger Military Archive, Army
Museum Waiouru, NZ)
black dog books thanks the Australian War Memorial, the Kippenberger Military
Archive, and the State Library of NSW for assistance with photographs, and the
Australian War Memorial for its kind assistance in reading the manuscript. Every
effort has been made to trace and acknowledge copyright material. The author
and publisher would be pleased to hear from any copyright holders who have not
been acknowledged.

National Library of Australia cataloguing-in-publication data:
Davidson, Leon, 1973- .
        Scarecrow army : the Anzacs at Gallipoli.
        For children aged 9+.
        ISBN 9781876372606.
        1. Australia. Army. Australian and New Zealand Army Corps -
        Juvenile fiction. 2. World War, 1914-1918 - Campaigns -
        Turkey - Gallipoli Peninsula - Juvenile fiction. I. Title.
        A823.4

10 9 8 7   10 11 12 13 14

To Clare, Robbie, Gaye and Michael, thank you.

Contents

Introduction

Before I wrote this book, I knew very little about Gallipoli. For me, Anzac Day was remembering the Second World War because my grandad was in it, and *Gallipoli* was an Australian movie starring Mel Gibson, without any New Zealanders in it. After researching Gallipoli, I'm glad to know more of our joint history, but saddened when I imagine the lives and dreams of those who were killed.

One New Zealand soldier, Gerald Sievers (whose story is told in the fiction sections), had paid for singing lessons and was accepted into the Italian Sistine Chapel choir. His father wouldn't let him go, so Gerald enlisted, only to be killed a year later in a desperate but futile battle. Who knows what could have happened if he'd survived. Unlike Gerald, Pete Walden is a fictional character, but his experiences are similar to those of many Anzacs I read about.

I often found it difficult to understand why the soldiers charged to certain death rather than disobey orders. Maybe it was because most of the men, at first, never believed that they'd die. Someone else would, but not them. Maybe it was because no one wanted to be seen as a coward or troublemaker. Maybe it was because they'd been raised not to question authority. They were also part of a much larger operation and disobeying an order could easily have resulted in the death of other men. One Australian soldier who'd been told he was too sick to fight, joined an attack and was shot. When asked why he'd taken part when he didn't have to, he replied, "If I had not stopped this, some other poor beggar would." The men were no longer individuals — they were part of an army, and their friends, other soldiers and their country relied on them.

Today Anzac Day is about remembering all military campaigns, not just Gallipoli. We don't look too deeply at why the Anzacs were at Gallipoli, we just blame it on the British, conveniently forgetting that Australian and New Zealand politicians and people willingly joined the war.

How many Australians and New Zealanders know that more British and French fought and died at Gallipoli than Anzacs? Or that the Anzacs didn't land at the wrong place as is commonly believed? History is always selective — you never hear the whole story — and there are many myths about Gallipoli.

One Anzac was asked as an old man how the war should be remembered. He said it shouldn't be, because eventually it would only be names and dates to people who couldn't imagine what it was really like. This is a story that's not just about names and dates, or myths, but about the lives of the Anzacs who fought there.

Chapter one –
A Man's World

What if you were there...
Anzac Cove, 25 April 1915.
I've just got to keep going, following these Australians. I'll find the others soon. It's bloody noisy. These bushes are a bastard. There's more bodies twisted up ahead – must have had bad luck. An explosion above. White smoke and cries of pain. I don't think I've ever seen such a blue sky. God, I'm already knackered.

"We need more men," someone shouts.

Something smacks me in the arm and I swivel to whack whoever's done it. My sleeve's torn and reddening. There's mangled flesh through the hole. Blood's dripping from my fingers onto the ground. I only just got up here. I haven't even seen a bloody Turk.

~

Wellington, August 1914.
Two years I've been working in the wool store and I've never been able to get the taste out of my mouth or the oil from my hands. I went as soon as I heard the news and a fair Wellington gale blew me into the recruiting office.

3

I stood like a fool as the doctors checked my mouth, and measured my weight and height. That was enough for them and I was chuffed when they told me I was in.

Now I'm number 10/87 and I'm finally going to do something with my life. Who would've believed it, me, a soldier marching off to war to help the Empire?

I wonder if Dad will try to stop me this time.

~

Wairarapa, August 1914.

I dance and shadow-box down the road and by the time I get home I'm full of beans, even though I know Mum's not going to take the news well. She doesn't even say hi when I burst in the front door and hand her the tea towels I got for her in Wellington.

"You're not going," are the first words she says. "It's their war, they started it, let them sort it out."

"King and Empire, Mum," I say, smiling.

"I won't let you go, Gerald."

"I'm 24. Anyhow it's too late, I've already been accepted."

"Go tell your dad — he's out the back." She doesn't take her eyes off me.

There's been a bit of rain and the lambs are getting fat on the grass. Dad's been working hard the last couple of months but the extra acres he's cleared have aged him and his back looks stiff as. Dad's pulling out a sheep's guts when I tell him I've signed up. He's still for a moment and

I've got no idea what he's thinking, then he says, "You sure you're doing the right thing?"

"I don't want to work in the wool store the rest of my life."

"German fools, picking a fight with all the world at once," is all he says as he turns back to the carcass.

It's hard trying to sleep with Mum and Dad bickering in the next room. Mum must've cooked her best roast ever tonight. Bugger-all had been said about me going, but my younger sisters and brothers were all keen to hear about what was happening in Belgium, and I'd rather remember us singing round the piano than this argument.

I can hear Mum saying, "You should've let him go to Italy."

"No son of mine is going to sing in a choir. Besides, this'll toughen him up, make a man out of him."

In the morning, my mum hugs me tightly and doesn't say a word as Dad grips my hand and says, "Make us proud, son."

"I will Dad, I will."

~

Palmerston North, Awapuni Racecourse, September 1914.
I'm bored with this training. We've been given uniforms and rifles, yelled at and marched from here to bloody

Timbuktu. And now we're outside this room, waiting to find out if we're gonna get knocked out.

"Sievers."

I go into the room and strip. My weight and height are measured again, another doctor tests my eyes by holding coloured wool in front of them, another man checks my hearing, and then someone holds my balls and says, "Cough." Then I have to jump around the room on one leg, then the other and finally they put a tick by my name. I get dressed, then leave the room. A couple of the lads are sent home. Glad it's not me, I'd hate to have to go back after having said goodbye to everyone.

~

Wellington, October 1914.
Finally we're marching through crowds of people waving Union Jacks and the drums are beating as hard as my heart. It feels grand. The wharf's packed and everyone's laughing and talking and hugging, but I'm glad Mum and Dad couldn't make it down. One man's girlfriend is pulled off by a cop because she wouldn't let go. We board the ships and crowd the sides to throw streamers and wave goodbye. I've never felt better in my life.

Gerald Sievers
Wellington Battalion
New Zealand Infantry Brigade

THE MARCH TO WAR
SARAJEVO, 28 JUNE 1914

It took two bullets fired from Gavrilo Princip's revolver to bring Europe to the brink of war. Archduke Franz Ferdinand, heir to the Austro-Hungarian throne, and his wife lay dead on the back seat of the Austrian royal car. They had been visiting Bosnia-Herzegovina, which was a relatively new province of Austria.

Twenty-year-old Princip was part of a political group that wanted Bosnia-Herzegovina to be part of Serbia, not the Austro-Hungarian Empire. In all, six men had been sent to kill the Archduke that day. After assassinating the Archduke, Princip put the revolver to his own head, but a passer-by grabbed him before he could pull the trigger. He never expected to live; he had been given cyanide tablets to take like all the other assassins.

Under interrogation, Princip confessed that important Serbian government officials were behind the assassination. Austria demanded that Serbia take action against those responsible, but they refused. On 28 July 1914, Austria declared war on Serbia, and began bombarding its capital, Belgrade.

Massive demonstrations against Austria spread across Russia. The Czar of Russia ordered the mobilisation of his forces to support Serbia. There was no way a wider European war could be stopped now.

Germany, Austria's ally, declared war on Russia and demanded that Russia's ally, France, remain neutral.

Gavrilo Princip
died in jail from
tuberculosis before
the end of the war.

France said it would follow its own interests, but when it started preparing to help Russia, Germany marched its army through neutral Belgium in an attempt to defeat the French before Russia had fully mobilised its massive army. In response, Britain declared war on Germany. The First World War had started.

HALF A WORLD AWAY

Although Australia and New Zealand were on the other side of the world, both countries closely followed the lead-up to war in Europe. They were both members of the British Empire, and the British Union Jack flag fluttered from flagpoles, and people sang the national anthem, "God Save the King". Many New Zealanders and Australians saw Britain — the 'mother country' — as 'home' even if they hadn't been there. Both countries did what Britain wanted: they introduced compulsory military training when Britain suggested it, and in 1912 New Zealand offered its new force to Britain if it wanted to seize German colonies in the Pacific. In 1914, both countries were quick to offer their armies to defend King and Empire.

On 31 July, Andrew Fisher, the opposition leader, told a meeting that "Australia will stand beside the mother country to help and defend her to our last man and our last shilling." The next night, Joseph Cook, the Prime Minister, said, "If there is to be war, you and I shall be in it. We must be in it. If the old country is at war, so are we." The British Empire had to be defended — it was New Zealand and Australia's main trading partner and without her the two countries would be alone in the Pacific.

Australia offered the British government 20 000 soldiers and its navy to be used wherever and however Britain desired. News of the offer was greeted with enthusiasm in Australia. In New Zealand, crowds marched waving Union Jack flags in support of Britain. Two days later, New Zealand offered 8000 men.

THE RUSH TO ENLIST

The day after war was declared, the first recruitment offices opened in Melbourne. Men from the cities queued from the early morning to enlist. Soon men began to arrive from the country. Not everyone was accepted — you had to be a certain height and have good teeth and feet. Those who were rejected were too embarrassed to look their mates in the eye as they left.

In Australia, men locked up houses and left farms

untended while they tried to enlist. One man who was rejected four times in Melbourne was eventually accepted in Sydney. Another rode 740 kilometres to Adelaide, then sailed to Hobart, before finally getting into the Light Horse in Sydney. Some men paid bribes. Like the Australians, the New Zealanders also went from city to city until they were taken. Old men shaved their faces to look younger and under-age men got their parents to write notes giving them permission to go to war.

The men who enlisted were at first mainly young and single. They came from the country and cities. There were farmers and teachers, lawyers and the unemployed. Most were looking for an adventure — they packed Kodak cameras to photograph parts of the world they'd never seen. Some signed up because all their mates had and it was the right thing to do. Others went to serve "King, Empire and Country". Those not enlisting tried to outdo each other in proving their patriotism — they sang "Rule Britannia" and waved Union Jack flags.

In Australia, you could volunteer from the age of 18 through to 35. In New Zealand it was from 20 to 34. The minimum age for the Ottoman army was 15.

As the war intensified, people from a German background were harassed and abused. Soon, many

German residents were interned in camps. Melbourne's St Kilda football club pinned Union Jacks on their tops because their team colours were the same as the German military flag. Not everyone believed in the war, but those opinions weren't popular and men who hadn't enlisted were abused in the streets.

The rush of volunteers in Australia was so great that three brigades of infantry were increased to four and the Light Horse from one to three. Four New Zealand districts — Otago, Canterbury, Wellington and Auckland — each provided an infantry battalion and a mounted rifle regiment.

The Australian commander, General William Bridges, wanted soldiers who knew and trusted each other, so he based battalions on states and districts. He wanted soldiers to know that their friends and neighbours were fighting beside them. In a way it was a form of peer pressure — men were less likely to disobey orders if it meant letting their mates down.

Women handed white feathers to men who hadn't enlisted. It was a way of saying they were cowards. In many cases, the men who were given feathers soon joined the army.

Men accepted into the Australian Light Horse and the New Zealand Mounted Rifles provided their own horse and saddle; the government provided everything else.

"In the evening, Mother, Father and sister Ada came down to see me off. We held a blue streamer between us until it snapped."

Harold Hinckfuss,
Australian Signaller,
26th Battalion.

Even though command of the two forces was handed over to Britain, New Zealand and Australia still had to pay for the transport of the troops, their food and ammunition. They were paying Britain to use New Zealanders and Australians however and wherever they wanted to, no questions asked.

The Australians were paid six shillings a day by their government, and became known as 'six bob a day tourists'. The New Zealanders were paid five shillings. The British soldiers only got one shilling a day.

On 29 August, New Zealand occupied 'German' Samoa without a shot being fired. The first German territory had fallen. Everyone believed it was going to be a short war. Britain, after all, was the greatest naval power in the world. The soldiers marched through cheering crowds to board their ships and throw streamers at family and friends on the wharves. The New Zealanders would travel further than any other country in history to fight this war. But first they had to meet up with the Australians in Albany, Western Australia.

THE OTTOMAN EMPIRE ENTERS THE WAR

In 1500 AD, the Ottoman Empire reached from Austria to Iran and covered most of the Middle East, but it had grown too vast. By the 1800s, it was losing territory to other countries and was being called "the sick man of Europe". By 1912, it consisted mainly of Turkey and parts of the Middle East. A group called the 'Young Turks' overthrew the Sultan in 1913 to prevent further disintegration. They took over government and started courting Britain and Germany — two of the major world powers — for support of their vulnerable regime. The Germans already understood Turkey's importance — it was the gateway to the Middle East and the riches of its oil fields. By 1913, Britain also wanted control of the oil fields, but they underestimated the Young Turks and continued to meet with members of the old regime.

At the beginning of August, Enver Pasa, the leader of the Young Turks, signed a secret alliance with a German diplomat. It guaranteed that Germany would help Turkey out in the event of war and Turkey would keep the Dardanelles strait — Russia's sea trading route — closed. With a war against Germany looming, Britain decided to keep two warships they had been building for the Turks — the Turkish people had donated most of their savings to have the warships built. So when Germany offered two of their own battlecruisers to the Young Turks, it was only a matter of time before

Turkey sided with Germany. Late in October, the battlecruisers, still under German command, left the Turkish capital Constantinople — now called Istanbul — and steamed north, attacking Russian ports. Russia declared war on Turkey and, several days later, British ships bombarded the Turkish forts guarding the entrance to the Dardanelles. On 5 November, Britain and France declared war on Turkey. The British and French armies were already fighting the Germans in France; now they had a new enemy.

STALEMATE ON THE WESTERN FRONT

By early December 1914, the trenches and barbed wire of the Western Front stretched from the Belgian coast across France to Switzerland. Nearly one million soldiers had already been killed and the Western Front had become a deadly stalemate. No one could break through the trenches and the lines wouldn't change by more than 16 kilometres until March 1918.

Looking for ways to get behind the Germans, Winston Churchill, Britain's First Lord of the Admiralty, drew up plans for the British navy to force their way up the Dardanelles strait to Constantinople. He believed the Young Turks would surrender at the first sight of British battleships. This would allow Russia to pull its troops back from the Turkish borders and then advance toward Germany in full force. This in turn would take the pressure off the British and French on the Western Front as Germany rushed its reinforcements to meet the Russians. Churchill was sure his plan would work. Years earlier, he had written a novel where warships destroyed coastal forts in a similar way and this seemed to have influenced his thinking.

But the Turks, knowing the British would attack again, fortified the hills and forts along both coasts of the 66-kilometre Dardanelles strait. They installed more heavy artillery and searchlights, dug trenches, placed barbed-wire entanglements on the shore, and laid 350 sea mines in the Narrows, the narrowest part of the strait.

TRYING TO FORCE THE DARDANELLES

On 19 February 1915, sailors on British battleships watched huge clouds of dust rising from the ancient Turkish forts they were bombarding. The campaign to knock Turkey out of the war had begun. But by dusk, several of the forts at the entrance were still firing back and bad weather had set in. A week

SIR WINSTON CHURCHILL: After being a soldier and journalist in India, Churchill was elected to Parliament in 1900 before heading the Admiralty in 1911. He fell out of favour after the Gallipoli fiasco, but went on to be Britain's Prime Minister during the Second World War.

15

later they tried again. This time the outer forts were silenced. The battleships steamed into the strait and started bombing the inner forts guarding the Narrows. Minesweepers tried to clear the sea mines but Turkish guns showered them with shells and the sailors refused to sweep until the forts and guns were destroyed.

British leaders started talking about a land invasion to destroy the forts so the sea mines could be safely cleared. In March, Sir Ian Hamilton — a British general — was sent from Britain to organise a landing on the Gallipoli peninsula. He arrived with two tourist books on Turkey, an inaccurate map and a textbook about the Ottoman army from 1905. While he was planning the land invasion the navy launched one last all-out attack. French and British battleships fired round after round and by 2 p.m. the Turks were running out of ammunition and their forts were almost destroyed. But then one of the ships suddenly exploded and sank rapidly with almost all its crew lost. The Turks had

SIR IAN HAMILTON: Commander-in-Chief of the land invasion of Gallipoli. Under his command were 75000 men, including the untested Australian and New Zealand Army Corps. Even though he'd served in numerous military campaigns he proved to be an indecisive commander.

laid 26 more sea mines the night before and soon two more battleships ran into them. The remaining ships retreated and the Turks celebrated. They had defeated the naval might of the British Empire; now they prepared for a land invasion they knew would surely be coming.

Gerald Sievers before he enlisted. (Patricia Lissienko)

Chapter two –
Sand and Pyramids

What if you were there...
Egypt, January 1915.
We're off down the narrow lanes, knocking over fruit stalls and whacking the donkeys hard to make them go faster. The Gyppo who rented us the donkeys is chasing us, yelling at us to slow down but he might as well be speaking French for all we care. Last one to the Wazza's got to buy all the drinks but I'm as skint as a Scotsman after being robbed last week.

"Imshi yalla," I yell back at him, but he's not gonna give up and let us have our fun. I reckon he knows we're gonna do a runner when we've finished racing. Come on you stupid elephant, I'm gonna lose if you don't start running.

Jimmy's just in front of me, but Mick's gonna win, even if he's only hanging on by the donkey's mane. If I've got any luck he'll fall off and be buying the rounds. I've known Mick forever, went to school and played cricket with him. He's keen on my young sis but I don't know how far he's got. I told her she'd be better off dancing with a Hun, but I was just joking.

18

"*Get outta the bloody way, fool!*" *I holler at some stuck-up British officer with a cane and looking glass. Must've given him a fright 'cos he's not saying anything as I trot past, saluting him. Then he starts barking at me. "You. You stop right now! Get back here, Private. I'll have you arrested."*

I'm about to tell him to shut his gob when our Gyppo friend knocks him over. Ha! He shouldn't be standing in the middle of the road. Good thing there's no Redcaps around or I'd have another stint in the lock-up tent.

I'd never been in trouble with anyone until I got to this dirty, sand-filled place. Must be Jimmy, he's always filling me with awful-tasting grog and leading me down the wrong streets. My dad would say he'd been right all along, that I am just a disappointment, but I blame the desert. Two months we've been here and it's been forced marches and drills every bloody day except Sunday and even then there's nothing to do but drink and make your own fun. The first week was okay, seeing the pyramids and checking out the ladies in the Wazza, but I didn't leave Australia to march under the hot sun without drinking water. Still, it's better than being in Albany gutting fish and being lectured by Mum and Dad. Somehow I've caught up to Jimmy and I say, "Hey, Jimmy, looks like your donkey's done its dash."

"He's no Melbourne Cup winner, Pete."

"No way we'll be paying the Gyppo for these nags."

I was hoping to overtake him but my donkey's just as bad. Then something hits the back of my head. The Gyppo's got his other shoe off and he throws it at us but it hits a man selling liquorice-water. It's bloody funny and Jimmy shouts, "Eggs-a-cook." That just winds the Gyppo up more but there's nothing he can do but wave his fist at us and get his shoe back.

"Hey Jim, the war's going to be over before we leave this place," I say cheekily, knowing Jimmy's horrified about that happening.

"It better bloody not be."

"I'll bet you two bob. How many times have we been shooting with bullets and not puffs of air? Not many and that's 'cos England's running out of ammo. They've got no bullets left so we've got to lose, don't we? We can't fight the Huns with pretend bullets can we?"

But Jimmy's not having any of it. He looks behind and says, "What's that?"

Apart from the Gyppo following us I can't see what he's on about. Then he shoves me off.

"Looks like you'll be shouting us," Jim says.

By the time I'm on my feet, the Gyppo's hitting me with his fists. He's a wiry bastard and he's angry and yelling, "You pay, you pay, three donkeys, you pay."

I wish he'd stop hitting me but I've got no money to give him and there's blood in my eye. I'm just glad Mick and Jimmy can't see me. Then I see a quick, sharp hook hit the Gyppo and he goes down. There's a New Zealander standing over him. He's not massive but he's got huge hands on him. No wonder the Gyppo's not getting back up.

"You beat me to it — couple more seconds and I would've had him."

"Sorry about that," he says.

"You're a Maorilander aren't you?" I ask.

"Yeah, that's what we're being called now."

"I'm Pete," I say. "From Australia."

"Yeah, I could tell that the minute I saw you," he says, grinning at me. "My name's Gerald Sievers. I'm from Wellington."

"That was one hell of a hook. You a boxer or something?"

"Used to be."

I haven't even got any money to buy him a drink, but being a Maorilander he'd probably turn his nose up at me so I just thank him and head to the Wazza to find Jimmy and Mick. I know I wanna get at the Germans, but I'll have to do better than that or else everything my dad says about me is gonna be true. Saved by a New Zealander, what a bloody disgrace.

Private Pete Walden
11th Battalion, 3rd Australian Infantry Brigade
1st Australian Division

LEAVING ALBANY

On 1 November 1914, the adventure began. Twenty-eight Australian and ten New Zealand ships pulled out of Albany, Western Australia, on their way to Britain to continue training. The soldiers had waited weeks for this moment — it wouldn't be long until they were at the Western Front fighting the German 'Hun'. Three cruisers escorted them to protect them from the German cruisers patrolling the oceans.

TRAPPED AT SEA

During the long hot days, the men trained. On some ships, they exercised the horses when the oceans were calm. Between training, they watched flying fish dart through the air and some men saw whales for the first time. Some of the soldiers were seasick, sometimes for weeks, and once someone vomited, it was hard for the man next to him to keep his lunch down. The men became bored and they tried to liven up their days with cricket, boxing competitions and concerts with bagpipes and pianos. "It's a long way to Tipperary" was a favourite but some Australians wanted a song about their own country.

There were 7843 horses on the Australian ships and 3815 on the New Zealand ships.

During the trip, the men were inoculated against typhoid. The injections were so painful that men had to wear slings afterwards. A rumour started that a soldier died from the shot, and some men refused the second injection, even though they knew they'd be sent home once the ships had docked.

The 11th Australian Battalion smuggled a kangaroo called 'Joey' on their ship to Egypt as a mascot.

But not all of the soldiers made it to dry land. When a ship slowed and pulled away from the convoy, the men knew a short church service was being held before a body was buried at sea.

On 28 November, they were told that they weren't going to Britain — not yet anyway. They would be trained in Egypt before being sent to the French battlefields. Britain needed them in Egypt to protect

NZ troops practising a haka on board the troopship "Maunganui".
(Kippenberger Military Archive, Army Museum Waiouru, NZ)

the Suez Canal, which was a vital trade route with India and Asia.

Even though the men were disappointed that they weren't going to be 'home' in Britain for a white Christmas, they were still excited about seeing the pyramids they'd learnt about at school. As the ships passed down the Suez Canal, Indian and Gurkha soldiers cheered them on. This was the British Empire they'd seen on maps and the men felt like heroes coming to Europe's aid.

EGYPT, 3 DECEMBER 1914

The convoy docked at Alexandria in the morning. The port was hectic and noisy. Egyptians ran up and down planks with buckets of coal on their heads to supply the ships. After being at sea for over a month the men were finally on land. They stretched their legs walking to the railway station where they were packed like sardines into long trains for the trip to Cairo. They were amazed by the Egyptian countryside. Irrigation canals crisscrossed the flat green land, fishermen threw nets from small boats, date

"Who are you?" called an Indian soldier as the New Zealand transport steamed down the Suez Canal. "We're New Zealanders," was the reply. "Hooray!" he called back. "Advance Australia!"

palms swayed in the wind, mud houses overflowed with people, chickens, goats, dogs and sheep. As the day grew dark and cold, there were outlines of pyramids in the distance.

India, like Australia and New Zealand, was also part of the British Empire and provided soldiers to help defend Britain.

The first troops arrived in Cairo at 1 a.m. and marched to their camps on the edge of a great desert. The horses, too weak to be ridden, panicked every time they saw a camel and the men had to use all their strength to stop them bolting. The New Zealanders camped at Zeitoun, the Australian Light Horse at Ma'adi, and the Australian Infantry at Mena, next to the pyramids. A small plantation of eucalypts at Mena reminded the Australians of home.

It was stinking hot by 9 a.m. and, as the men roasted under the sun, Lancashire Territorials — British soldiers — welcomed them with smokes, cups of tea and "summat t' eat". The Australians and New Zealanders were huge next to the Lancashire men. The more they chatted with the British the more they realised how different they were.

The soldiers put up large canvas tents and the camps began to look like small towns. The streets running between the rows of tents were given New Zealand and Australian names. This was now their new home.

They were bitten by mozzies and the hard sand was so uncomfortable they scooped out hippies and made sand pillows. Sand got into everything — blankets, ears, noses and food. They hoped they wouldn't be there too long, or the war could be over without them. But the weeks dragged into months.

A DAY OF REST

The soldiers started training immediately. They marched and practised manoeuvres across the never-ending desert and fought an invisible enemy. They exercised the horses. The artillery fired at dummy targets. Their packs, loaded with gear, weighed 36 kilograms. One soldier, Private Harold Cavill of the 2nd Australian Battalion, felt like his legs were being pulled out with each step. The soldiers trained six days a week and had Sundays off. They had a lot to learn and they wanted to prove they were as good as the British Tommy. Some days they trained for over ten hours. Those with bad knees or weak chests were weeded out and sent home. They were devastated even if the training was killing them.

On their Sundays off, the soldiers wrote letters home, climbed the pyramids and cut their names next to those of Roman and Napoleonic soldiers. Men had their photos taken on camels with the sphinx in the background and went roller-skating at rinks in Cairo and Heliopolis. They also had boxing matches and looted old archaeological sites for treasures. Church services were held and thousands of voices filled the desert.

A. & N. Z. A. C.

After several weeks, Lord Kitchener, Britain's Secretary of State for War, combined the New Zealand and Australian forces into an Army Corps. It needed a name and "Australasian Army Corps" was the first suggestion, but the New Zealanders didn't want to be dwarfed by Australia. Australian and New Zealand Army Corps was chosen and a stamp was made using the initials A.& N.Z.A.C., which became known as the Anzac stamp. The headquarters staff used the word 'Anzac' regularly but it took a long time for the soldiers to use it. Many didn't even know it on the day they landed at Gallipoli.

The Anzac Corps was made up of two divisions — the Australian Division which consisted of the 1st, 2nd and 3rd Australian Infantry Brigade, and the New Zealand and Australian Division which consisted of the New Zealand Infantry Brigade, the New Zealand Mounted Rifle Brigade, the 1st Australian Light Horse Brigade and the 4th Australian Infantry Brigade. The 2nd and 3rd Australian Light Horse Brigades were not in either division but were still Corps troops.

THE WAZZA

The men soon became bored and frustrated with fighting mock battles in the desert. They were never going to get to the Western Front at this rate.

Some decided that if the army wasn't going to give them an adventure they'd find their own. The roads to and from Cairo became jammed with vehicles. Roofs and footboards of trams were crowded with soldiers and every day more troops poured into Cairo than had permission to go. One tram was so overcrowded that it came off the tracks. This hiccup didn't stop the Australians. They just piled off and lifted the tram back on. It was in Cairo that the New Zealanders and Australians started to see and dislike each other's differences. They bickered and got into rowdy arguments. Even before the transports had left Australia, the New Zealanders were comparing themselves to the Australians. The New Zealanders believed they were more disciplined and that their uniforms were better.

Egyptian businesses welcomed the soldiers — they were great replacements for the American tourists who'd stayed at home because of the war. Soon Egyptian restaurants and pubs carried New Zealand and Australian names — 'Wellington Hotel – very cheap and breezy', 'All Blacks' and 'Kangaroo Café'.

The soldiers were pestered by young bootblacks

desperate to clean their already spotless boots: "Bootsa clean sir, no good, no money, Kiwi polish sir!" Unable to cope, the soldiers would kick them away. Most of the Australians and New Zealanders treated the Egyptians badly, at times robbing and beating them. They called them 'Gyppos'. Although they were both bigoted, the Australians thought the New Zealanders were too soft on the Egyptians. They believed this was because of the respect the New Zealanders had for the Maoris.

The Ezbekieh quarter — the 'Wazza'— a red-light district filled with bars and brothels, became very popular. Many of the men spent most of their money and time there. Some stopped going back to their camps at all. Alcohol was cheap and it soon looked like the Anzacs were in danger of becoming an army of drunks. Hundreds were hospitalised with syphilis and other sexually transmitted diseases. The British officers already believed that one British soldier was better than three Anzacs. An army of crippled drunks wasn't going to change that opinion.

TOEING THE LINE

General Alexander Godley tried to fix the problem by encouraging the New Zealanders to stay away from the Australians. They were urged to stay sober and dress neatly to prove that New Zealand was the better country of the two. This worked, even if it did drive a wedge between the New Zealanders and Australians. Some Australians thought the New Zealanders were boring and poor imitations of themselves, while New Zealanders thought the Australians were arrogant and loud. Not everyone felt this way — there were still Australians and New Zealanders who became friends.

Godley knew he couldn't stop his men getting drunk or visiting brothels altogether, so he set up canteens in the camps and treatment centres to prevent more men getting sick. It was kept a secret because Godley knew the New Zealand public would be outraged. The men who didn't change were shipped back home and their name and the reason for their dismissal were printed in the New Zealand newspapers. They were disgraced — the laughing stock of New Zealand. The strategy worked. The men began following every order.

SIR ALEXANDER GODLEY: New Zealand Commander. British-born Godley was good with training and discipline, but not at leadership on the battlefield. He rarely praised his men and recommended few for medals. He became widely disliked by the New Zealand troops.

There were far more Australians than New Zealanders in Egypt and their commander, Major General Bridges, was slower to crack down on them. By January, more than 300 soldiers were absent without leave. Men rampaged through the streets of Cairo. Not everyone was a troublemaker but the men stuck together. If someone got in trouble, others helped him out. One night General William Birdwood's car was stolen from out the front of his headquarters in Cairo and was found the next morning, abandoned in the middle of the Australian Mena camp.

It got so bad that Birdwood wrote to Bridges telling him to discipline his troops. Like Godley, Bridges sent the worst offenders home and instructed Charles Bean, the official Australian correspondent stationed with the troops, to write to the newspapers at home explaining why. The threat of humiliation finally worked and the Australians toed the line. Canteens and treatment centres were opened in the camps. Men would queue for miles before being given one bottle of beer, then they'd sneakily queue for another. But it was too late for their reputation — Australian soldiers would always be known as larrikins.

GENERAL WILLIAM BIRDWOOD: Commander of the Anzacs. Got on with the Anzacs better than most British officers. The Anzacs nicknamed him 'Birdy'. He swam with the men at Anzac Cove and visited them at the front-line but would always refuse cups of tea as he didn't want to drink their precious water.

MAJOR GENERAL WILLIAM BRIDGES: Australian Commander. Bridges was admired by the soldiers because he toured the front-lines every day, walking and standing under heavy fire when most would have ducked. He was the first Australian general to be killed, shot by a Turkish sniper on 15 May.

In early February, two months after they arrived in Egypt, the New Zealanders finally fought a real enemy. A Turkish army had marched and dragged boats over the Sinai desert to attack Egypt. The New Zealanders with the Indians and British lined the eastern banks of the Suez Canal. The Turkish soldiers were exhausted when they arrived and during the night they tried to cross the canal in boats. Many were shot before they'd even reached the water's edge. Sixteen hundred Turkish men and 160 British Empire soldiers died. One of them was Private William Ham, New Zealand's first casualty of the First World War. But it had been an easy victory. The Anzacs were convinced they'd easily beat the Turks again if they were given the chance.

FAREWELL EGYPT

After the Anzacs paraded for Sir Ian Hamilton and were pronounced ready for active service, many Anzacs suspected they'd soon be fighting the Turks.

They didn't mind as long as it was just a quick warm-up before getting at the 'Hun'. On Good Friday, the soldiers were given day passes and many headed to the Wazza to celebrate. After drinking all day, a fight broke out in one of the pubs after a rumour spread that a New Zealand soldier had been stabbed. Soon the Wazza was being torn to pieces. They dragged whatever they could find from the bars, or threw things from the balconies — furniture, beds, even a piano — and set them on fire. When the Egyptian fire fighters arrived, they were beaten back by more than 2000 soldiers. Redcaps ran in to break up the crowd, but had to flee from bottles being thrown at them. The celebrations were short-lived. A regiment of Lancashire Territorials lined the streets with rifles and bayonets and the men, knowing what was best for them, headed back to their camps.

LEAVING EGYPT, 9 APRIL 1915

After four and a half months of training, the soldiers boarded boats for Lemnos, a Greek island 160 kilometres off the coast of Gallipoli. The New Zealand Mounted Rifles and Australian Light Horse were left behind because their horses would be no good on the Gallipoli peninsula. They were disappointed — nobody wanted to miss out. At Lemnos there was more training. They practised beach landings and climbed up and down rope ladders from ships into rowboats with their heavy packs and rifles. The weather was lovely, the landscape treeless. Hundreds of boats were anchored near the harbour; battleships, trawlers, ocean liners, submarines and torpedo boats. It was an amazing sight and everyone felt like they were part of something epic. By now the Anzacs knew they were going to invade Turkey. And the Turks knew they were coming — German planes had been seen flying over Lemnos. They just didn't know the exact day or time, but they prepared for it.

A German general, Liman von Sanders, had been given command of the Ottoman army at Gallipoli. He oversaw the soldiers' training and organised the formidable defence of the peninsula. He had trenches deepened and barbed wire entanglements put in the sea and along beaches where 'the English' were likely to land. About 500 Germans served on the peninsula, and the most active were a machine-gun unit from the German battlecruiser given to the Turks.

THE PLAN TO KNOCK OUT THE TURKS

The army's job was to destroy the forts protecting the Narrows so it could be safely cleared of mines. Then British and French ships could steam up the Dardanelles to Constantinople. The Anzacs were given what was considered the easiest part of the campaign because they were colonials, untested civilian-soldiers who might one day, after enough training, be as good as the British soldiers. The hard work would go to the British 29th Division who would land at Cape Helles, at the tip of the Gallipoli peninsula before making their way up the peninsula to the Kilid Bahr Plateau, a hill overlooking the Narrows. French soldiers, after landing on the Turkish mainland to draw attention away from the peninsula, would then land and support the British at Cape Helles. The Anzacs would land further north at Gaba Tepe in the dark, without a naval bombardment, and use the element of surprise to capture the heights of Hill 971 before moving to Mal Tepe, another hill above the Narrows. It was their job to block Turkish reinforcements getting to the British, who would be destroying the forts. The plan was very ambitious and relied heavily on surprising the Turks, and the belief that Turks were third-rate soldiers.

MIDNIGHT, 24 APRIL 1915

The ships lifted their anchors. British, French, and Australian and New Zealand ships pulled away from the harbour. They were off to war. No one thought they were going to die. They'd been told it would be easy. Someone had painted an arrow and "To Constantinople and the Harem" on the front of one of the boats. It was going to be over in 72 hours. That was the plan.

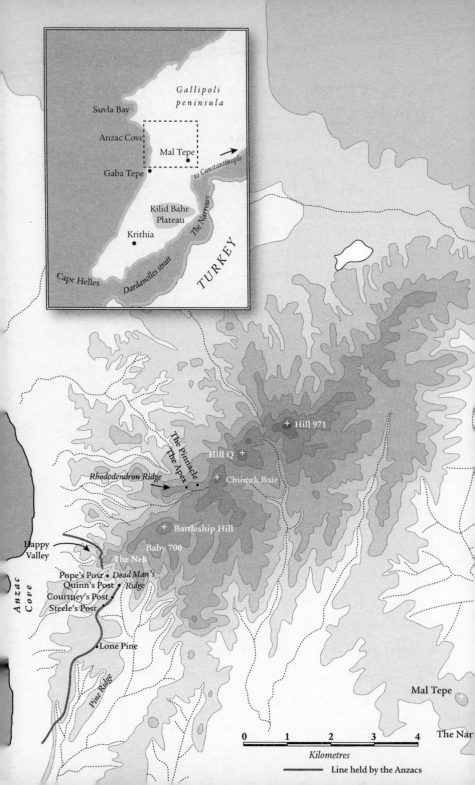

Gallipoli peninsula

Suvla Bay

Anzac Cove

Mal Tepe

Gaba Tepe

to Constantinople

Kilid Bahr Plateau

The Narrows

Krithia

Dardanelles strait

Cape Helles

TURKEY

Hill 971

Hill Q

The Pinnacle
The Apex

Rhododendron Ridge

Chunuk Bair

Battleship Hill

Baby 700

Happy Valley

The Nek

Pope's Post

Quinn's Post

Dead Man's Ridge

Courtney's Post

Steele's Post

Anzac Cove

Lone Pine

Pine Ridge

Mal Tepe

The Nar

| 0 | 1 | 2 | 3 | 4 |

Kilometres

Line held by the Anzacs

Chapter three —
For King and Empire

What if you were there...
Aegean Sea, 25 April 1915.

What am I doing here? No way I wanna be in this boat crammed with 40 tobacco stinking soldiers and the sun not even up. For weeks I've been waiting for this day to arrive. Now I don't know why I was so impatient. Only signed up 'cos they were paying six shillings a day. That's nearly twice as much as what I got for gutting fish and now I don't have to listen to my boss saying, "You should be doing 20 every ten minutes." On my last day I asked him why he wasn't signing up and that shut him up good. Ma was pretty happy, said she was proud of me, which is a change 'cos she's normally on me case about being 19 and not getting married, but it's not easy to get a girl when you stink of fish.

The boats pulling us to the shore are too bloody loud and the Turks must've heard us by now. Might as well have a brass band playing. My chances of getting married aren't too flash now but at least I danced with the ladies at the Wazza. Six shillings a day seemed like a lot when I signed up. Dad said I wasn't man enough to hold a rifle but who cares what that boozehead's got to say? Not only could I march the best out of the company but I'm a crack shot as well. It doesn't matter though, Dad's right, I'm not a man. I don't want to be here. I can't even swim.

Everyone's watching the black cliffs in front of us. I must be the only one who's scared to death. I've got hold of my rifle to hide my shaking hands but the gun's moving like a flag in the wind. Jimmy's looking at me. I hope he doesn't know that I don't want to be here.

"You looking forward to some fun, Pete?"

"Yeah, thought it'd never come," I answer.

"We'll do alright. Be easier than gutting fish."

"And paid twice as much."

Jimmy looks at the cove getting closer. The Tommies in charge reckon it's gonna be an easy fight, a cakewalk, whatever that means. They reckon the Turks will run when they see us. We've had a few bets about it. I said it'd be over in a day, that's what I hope anyway. But if they weren't any good, how'd they destroy all those ships? They won't run. Where are they gonna go? It's their country. Just about everyone's looking at the land getting closer.

Mick's up the front. He wants to kill the first Turk he told me. He's not afraid. He shook my hand before we climbed into this bathtub of a boat and said "good luck".

There's a muffled crack up in the hills. It could've been a gunshot.

Jimmy whispers, "You hear that?"

"Yeah. You reckon it's the Turks?"

"Could be."

Everyone's heard it. They all seem excited. Someone says he's finally gonna get to shoot a Turk.

Then they start shooting.

Someone says the bullets sound just like little birds and most of us laugh. Even I laugh. My face is warm. It's covered in Jimmy's blood. He's lying on me, deader than a fish. I push him off me and he thuds onto the bottom of the boat. I've just gotta do my best. What happened to Jimmy won't happen to me.

Private Pete Walden
11th Battalion, 3rd Australian Infantry Brigade
1st Australian Division

A COLD NIGHT, 25 APRIL 1915

The fleet sliced through the calm Aegean Sea. At
1 a.m. the soldiers were woken by sailors and given cups
of hot cocoa. The night was cold but it didn't matter.
The moment they'd all been waiting for had finally
arrived. The day before they'd laughed and joked while
sharpening their bayonets. Now they thought about
home. As empty bullet boxes floated in the sea below,
the men wrote letters to their families just in case. Mist
hung over the sea and the moon was nearly full.

The Australian soldiers slung their heavy packs on
and climbed down rope ladders with their rifles in hand
into a line of rowboats. It was quiet except for their
backpacks creaking and the dull thuds of rifle butts
on the deck. At 3 a.m. the moon disappeared behind
clouds. Twelve steamboats towed 36 rowboats towards
Gallipoli, filled with 1500 soldiers of the 3rd Australian
Brigade, men from Queensland, South Australia and
Western Australia. As dawn arrived the men could see
the dark shape of land. The steamboats cast them off
and they began to row to shore. There wasn't much
talking. They were nervous, wondering if the Turks
could see them. It was too quiet for their liking. Some
men wished the shooting would start — anything to
break the silence.

When they got close, the land looked different from
the gentle slope they were expecting. Soon a few soldiers

were sure they were too far north and heading for the wrong place. But it was too late. A small light glowed in the hills for 30 seconds. Everyone watched where the light had been and someone saw the shape of a man on the skyline. They kept rowing. Suddenly hundreds of Turkish rifles were firing; the hills sparkled with their flashes. The men were almost relieved. It had begun.

Men on the transports rushed on deck to see the action but it was too dark. All they could do was listen to the growing rifle fire. The New Zealanders couldn't believe the Australians were going to land before them — as if they weren't arrogant enough already. Barely 200 Turkish men waited for the Australians. They lay in shallow rifle pits and crouched in trenches with machine guns, knowing that Turkish reinforcements were coming.

A MOMENT OF GLORY

The first boat scraped onto the unnamed cove at 4.29 a.m. and the Australians piled into the cold sea. They waded to shore as bullets whistled past them. A few men fell before they'd even reached the stony beach. At the back of the boats the water was too deep and some men drowned, unable to remove their heavy packs, unnoticed by friends rushing up the beach to take cover behind a bank as Turkish bullets struck sparks off the stones.

Nothing was going to plan — their uniforms were soaked and rifles clogged with dirt. In front of them were eroded gullies, steep hills covered with waist-high scrub and small cliffs. Their orders were to push on at all costs and secure the higher ridges so the 1st and 2nd Australian Brigades could advance further inland to seize the heights above the Narrows. They weren't allowed to use bullets before dawn in case they shot another Australian by accident, so they fixed bayonets to the end of their rifles, threw off their packs and charged up the steep banks.

Full of adrenaline, the soldiers overran shallow Turkish trenches and bayoneted the men in them. For some, the rush of killing was intoxicating. They charged on, grabbing the branches and roots to pull themselves up, only to be shot by men they couldn't see. The wounded and dead rolled down the banks until they were caught in the scrub. Surrendering Turks were shot. Soldiers still on the beach cleaned grit from their rifles and shot into the hills, often into the backs of their own comrades. Turkish troops further north fired their machine guns at the rowboats carrying the 7th Australian Battalion. When the boats scraped onto the beach, most of the men were wounded or dead.

Four thousand Australians were now on the peninsula, and the Turks, now outnumbered, retreated, hiding in the thick scrub and picking off the Australians as they went. The Australians chased them and became broken up by the thick bush and tangle of gullies. Then Turkish shrapnel shells started bursting above the beaches and over the hills. The bombs exploded in clouds of white, metres above the land, spitting shrapnel pellets into the men below. The battleships returned fire and the morning was filled with the booming of the big naval guns. For the men on the ships it seemed impossible that anyone would live through such a bombardment.

A SNIFF OF VICTORY

By 7 a.m. the battle seemed more than half over. The Turks were fleeing. Men on the transports could see the Australians walking along the ridge, digging trenches, and sitting on their packs, smoking. Many of the Australians thought they'd done what was required of them. Lieutenant Colonel Ewan Sinclair-MacLagan, commander of the 3rd Australian Brigade, realised that his broken-up battalions couldn't secure the heights, so he disobeyed original orders and told his men to dig in. But few understood how important his order was and the digging of trenches on the Nek and along the second ridge was slow.

Others didn't know about Sinclair-MacLagan's orders. They kept pushing inland. One group made it far enough to see the Narrows. No Anzacs would make it this far again. Another group, led by Captain Eric Tulloch, of the 11th Battalion, chased the retreating Turks up the Second Ridge towards Battleship Hill.

For the next few hours, Australian soldiers were ferried onto Gallipoli and by 9 a.m., 12 000 were on the peninsula. The New Zealanders wanted to be with them. Few thought they'd see any action on the first day and now it seemed that the battle was going to be over before they'd even landed. The night before, men had laid bets on how soon they'd be in Constantinople. Most of them thought three days and this early success seemed to prove them right. But thousands of Turkish soldiers, with mule trains carrying artillery, were marching up a ridge to position themselves above the Australians.

"We were given orders to dig in. I was on the shovel and a fellow named Fred Adams was on the pick. He got shot through the forehead and died instantly."

Bill Groves, 8th Australian Battalion.

THE TIDE TURNS

Mustafa Kemal, the Turkish commander of the area, sent all the soldiers of his 19th Division to reinforce the troops already fighting the Australians. He wasn't meant to, but he was certain that the Australian landing was a major attack and not a diversion for the British at Cape Helles. He raced on horseback ahead of the reinforcements to Battleship Hill and watched a "hunter line of the enemy" rushing towards him. At one stage it looked like the Australians would reach him before his own men arrived. He stopped the fleeing Turkish troops and demanded to know why they were leaving. It didn't matter that they'd run out of ammunition, Kemal ordered them to fix bayonets and lie down to face the Australians.

In response, the Australians took cover and crept forward. Then the Turkish reinforcements arrived and their heavy fire pinned down the Australians. Turkish bullets ripped up the hard holly scrub and the prickly leaves got under their clothes. The men could barely see more than two soldiers on either side because of the thick bushes, let alone the Turks that were shooting at them. Captain Tulloch saw a Turkish officer giving orders as he stood under the only tree on Battleship Hill. It was probably Kemal but Tulloch's bullet missed him.

THE NEW ZEALAND REINFORCEMENTS

The New Zealanders stood on the decks of their transports listening to a church service. It was difficult to hear the padre over the thunder of the naval guns. The soldiers were full of praise for the Australians struggling up the hills. They watched the rowboats

Part of the 4th Battalion and mules landing at 8 a.m.
(AWM J03022)

At the water's edge lies an Australian engineer, Sapper Fred Reynolds, who was one of the first to die on the Gallipoli peninsula.

returning from the beach, envious of the wounded who'd seen action. Many of the wounded were in good spirits, but disappointed that it had ended so quickly. Others just wanted a cigarette. Blood collected in pools in the bottom of their boats.

The New Zealanders climbed down into the boats — the chance had finally arrived to show what they were made of. They sat, rifles between their legs, smoking and gazing up at the hills. It was almost 10 a.m. As the boats got closer, they could see soldiers cutting tracks into the steep banks and exhausted men sleeping on the beach as shrapnel burst above them. A soldier with a leg missing was being piggybacked down onto the beach. The beach was crowded with the wounded and the dying. Blankets covered the dead. Rifles, packs and letters littered the ground. Dead faces stared up from under the still water and men stumbled over the bodies as they waded to the shore. Some New Zealanders were reminded of the rugged hills back at home.

They were rushed up to help the thinning Australian line, sent to the left only to be sent to the right by another officer. The banks were so steep that stronger men pulled others up by their rifle barrels. Some of the men got lost in the gullies and others were directed to areas that were in urgent need of reinforcements. The day was already getting hot and they weren't allowed to drink their water until night and even then they had to ask permission. Each man's water bottle was meant to last three days. It was total confusion — Australians took orders from New Zealand officers and vice versa. The differences and petty arguments that had existed in Egypt disappeared as they fought beside each other.

Eventually many New Zealanders made their way up a gully littered with discarded packs, dead soldiers, mules and wounded men stumbling back to the beach. It was hot and the men were sweating heavily. Men lay quietly amongst the bushes, blank-eyed. The smell of wild thyme was everywhere. It was spring and poppies grew in sheltered places. Vultures flew overhead.

THE TURKS DIG THEIR HEELS IN

By 10 a.m. Kemal's counterattack was building and only a few of the Australians that had pushed inland made it back. Most were picked off or got lost in the gullies as they pulled back to a hill named Baby 700, where the New Zealanders joined them. The Anzacs knew this height had to be held or else the Turks would have a commanding view of the valleys below. Kemal, also knowing the hill's importance, told his men, "I am not ordering you to attack: I am ordering you to die. By the time we die other troops and commanders can take our place."

Anzac soldiers took ammunition from the dead and felt ashamed about taking cover behind corpses as they held off the ever-increasing Turkish fire.

By 10.30 a.m. the guns of the Indian Mountain Artillery had landed to support the Anzacs. The guns were carried on the backs of mules up the rugged slopes. It took the gunners ten minutes to assemble each gun, fire six shots, then repack the mules. They'd always try to move to a new location before the Turkish guns found them. The sound of the Indian guns was a relief to the men, but the Turks soon drove them out of action.

All across the hills, the wounded called for stretcher-bearers and water. That was what the soldiers hated the most — hearing the wounded calling for water. They could do nothing to help them. Some men just lay and talked to their dead friends. Other soldiers took personal possessions to send back to the dead man's family.

MUSTAFA KEMAL PASHA: Kemal's determined defence of Gallipoli resulted in great loss of Turkish life, but he is widely credited with defeating the British and saving the Dardanelles.

After the end of the war in 1918, Kemal led a war to keep all that was left of the Ottoman Empire, (mainly Turkey), intact. He became Turkey's first president in 1924, serving until his death. In 1934, he was given the title "Atatürk" – "Father of the Turks".

In one gully, an Australian and a New Zealander were found holding each other. Both men were dead.

The stretcher-bearers bandaged wounds as best they could and slipped morphine pills under tongues to dull pain. In steeper places it took hours to get the wounded to the beach. Even soldiers who should have been fighting helped the wounded down and then often got lost getting back. Private John Simpson, of the 3rd Field Ambulance, found a donkey and used it to bring wounded soldiers down from the front-line. He worked with little rest until he was killed bringing back two wounded soldiers on 19 May. Soon there was a steady stream of wounded soldiers limping down the gullies to the beach. Men tried to keep a brave face and those with less serious wounds would joke, "It's hot as hell up there." They were taken out to the hospital ships on the barges that had brought them in. Lightly wounded men gave up their places to the worse off, but some men rushed into the sea to get on the overcrowded boats. They were taken on board, but nobody liked them much.

The hospital ships filled up quickly and the boats of wounded went from ship to ship until they found one with enough room to take the soldiers on board. Some boats didn't have beds and the men had to use life jackets for pillows. Men died because there weren't enough doctors. On one ship the closest thing to a doctor was a vet who did his best for the dying men. On another ship, the sole doctor worked for 36 hours without sleep. Before night fell, the hospital ships left for Cairo.

THE ANZACS HOLD ON

There was every possibility that the Turks were going to defeat the Anzacs. No soldiers were landed between 12.30 and 4 p.m. and most of the New Zealanders and the Australian 4th Brigade were still on the boats. On land, the soldiers were defending two ridges two kilometres in length. They couldn't advance and, with the sea behind them, couldn't retreat.

A popular Turkish story says that at one spot a white cloth was raised and a Turkish soldier got out of his trench without his rifle. He gently picked up a wounded Anzac, carried him to the Anzac's trench and laid him down before returning to his own men. No one fired a shot.

The Anzacs on shore, lay in the scrub, shooting at wherever they thought the Turks might be. They couldn't dig for cover because they were shot when they stood up, so they lay there, desperately fighting for their lives, waiting for dark. Baby 700 changed hands five times, but by the end of the day the Anzacs were forced off. The Turks bayoneted the wounded soldiers left lying unnoticed in the bushes when they retook the hill.

NIGHT FINALLY ARRIVES

As night fell the Anzacs dug trenches up two narrow ridges to the Nek, a point below Baby 700. Most of the trenches were shallow but better than nothing. The land near the Nek and between the two ridges was eroded and inaccessible, except at a few points, which became Anzac outposts. The firing line was broken by gullies and nowhere was secure, let alone safe.

One of these outposts became known as Quinn's Post. Stragglers and reinforcements arrived and during the night the number of men rose to 150. They crept out under the cover of darkness and dragged the wounded back in. Across the rest of the Anzac line, the digging of trenches was frantic and exhausting. Most soldiers had been up since midnight and hadn't had anything to eat. To top it off, it started raining.

Reinforcements trudged up the valleys, passing soldiers boiling tea in mess tins over small fires and an endless stream of wounded coming down the hills. Men searched for shovels and picks that had been dropped earlier in the day. At that moment they were more important than guns.

Worn-out and leaderless men left the firing line and made their way back to the beach. Most were

STRETCHER-BEARERS:
A number of privates
in each company
were stretcher-
bearers and would
run out with their
stretchers, exposing
themselves to rifle
fire and shrapnel.
The volunteers wore
armbands and didn't
carry rifles and
although the Turks,
for the better
part, didn't shoot
at them, many were
still killed. Often
they worked until
they dropped from
exhaustion.

ordered back to the front, while others lay down and slept until woken and sent back. The beach was piled with hastily dumped boxes of bully beef, ammunition and biscuits. Lights from lanterns reflected off the wet stones where surgeons cared for the wounded. Above them, soldiers cut steps into the steep hills and made tracks up to the firing line.

Most of the Anzac leaders wanted to retreat but Hamilton, commander of the Gallipoli expedition, told them that they'd done the hardest part; and until the British arrived from Cape Helles they should just hold on and "Dig, dig, dig, until you are safe". It was the only direct order he gave since the landing, and that was in the early morning of 26 April. All of Hamilton's fears that the Anzacs weren't up to the task required were proving to be true. Sixteen thousand Australians and 3100 New

Zealanders were now on the peninsula. Across the ridges, 12 000 Turkish soldiers waited for dawn.

It was a cold, miserable night and it didn't stop raining. Men pulled heavy coats off the dead for extra warmth. They waited all night for a massive attack but the Turks could only manage small attacks. Before charges they would shout, "Allah!" and "Mohammed!" The Anzacs were always ready for them.

If the Anzacs had landed further south, they might have met barbed wire and machine guns like the British had at Cape Helles. At one beach at Helles the sea turned red with blood. With the sun already up, the British had grounded a ship in the shallows and men had poured out of doors cut in the side, straight into the paths of machine guns. At other beaches the men got entangled in submerged wire and were slaughtered by the Turks who'd returned to their trenches after the navy bombardment had finished. The soldiers who'd made it safely ashore at other places waited without orders. It was a delay they couldn't afford and Hamilton was failed by his generals who did not use their initiative.

Chapter four –
Ours Not to Reason Why, Ours But to Do and Die

What if you were there...
Anzac Cove, late May 1915.

The sun's starting to bite the back of my neck as we start heading into the cove. I hope I'm here a bit longer this time 'cos I don't want to be wounded again.

That hospital ship would easily be the worst week of my life. It was cramped, people were groaning, and it stank of piss. How any of us survived is a mystery. Once we got to Egypt, some English cow expected us to lie at attention in our beds every time she came into the room even though we were half dead. When I finally got out and about I spent my time checking the casualty lists for names of friends and getting my shoes shined four or five times a day. It was stinking hot but the one time I went for a swim a few soldiers' bodies were floating in the waves. They'd probably died on the hospital ships before we'd reached

Egypt and been buried at sea. Fish had eaten their eyes.

We step onto the wooden pier and we're quickly moved along. The place has changed and it smells like rotting sheep. The hills have got holes all over them and I'm sure there was a lot more scrub on the first day. There's men walking around and others sunbaking on the beach. If it wasn't for the crack of rifles you wouldn't know there was a war on. I'm sent left and I make my way up a steep track and run across open areas when told to. I feel like an idiot sprinting for my life when I've got no idea what I'm dodging. I find my platoon on front-line duty and it's great to be back with them. We shake hands till they're about to fall off and then light our Woodbines.

"It's a shame there's no billy on for you, Gerald."

"I don't need one. They spoilt me rotten in hospital."

"Any good-looking nurses, Gerald?" asks Reggie.

"All in good time. All in good time. Where's Harry?"

"He lost a leg a couple of weeks back," Reggie says.

"And James?" I ask.

"We haven't seen him since the landing."

"Jeez, we've been knocked up," I say.

There's a murmur of agreement and then no more is said. It's a shame about James, I thought he'd be alright. It looks like things haven't improved since the day I got knocked. We're still stuck on the same piece of land we got on the first day but at least now we've got trenches. I'm put to work pretty quickly and it's not long till I'm bored.

I've been watching the Turkish lines for the last hour or two and all I've seen is shovelled dirt being flung into the air. It's hot. It stinks and flies are living off my sweat.

"Where're the Turks digging to?"

"We reckon either under us or to China."

"Bloody hope it's China," I reply.

A Turk climbs out of his trench. I look again, then quickly slide back the bolt, take aim and fire. He rolls and comes to rest against a bush. I can't see much of him apart from his arm and legs but he's not moving. It's the first Turkish man I've ever seen. It was a good shot, even if he's a lot bigger than a rabbit.

"Did you get him," says Reggie.

"Nah, missed by a mile."

"Better luck next time, eh."

I don't know why I lied, but I can't get the Turk out of my head. I watch him for a while, wanting him to move. It's what I'm here to do but I keep thinking about my older brother and I feel terrible. I don't know a thing about the Turk. I wonder what his name is. I wished I hadn't done it but there's no point thinking like that. He's dead and there's nothing I can do about it. He shouldn't have stood up.

Gerald Sievers
Wellington Battalion
New Zealand Infantry Brigade

TUCKERED OUT, 26 APRIL 1915

As the sun rose on 26 April, the Anzacs lay down their picks and shovels, picked up their rifles and waited for the Turks to charge down the hills. But nothing happened. The Turks were also exhausted. At first, the Anzacs didn't waste their time digging deep trenches; they were still convinced that the British would defeat the Turks at Cape Helles and come to Anzac. Besides, they were shattered. They dozed in the trenches and rolled the dead over the steep sides of their posts into the gullies below because there wasn't time or energy to bury them. Already the bodies were beginning to smell.

The Turks spent the day regrouping and collecting rifles and equipment. Later that night their reinforcements started to arrive. They massed close to the front and waited. The next day they charged down Battleship Hill to throw the invaders off their land. They came in ordered lines, wave after wave, spread out across the hill. Most of the Australians and New Zealanders hadn't slept for three days. Some panicked and tried to run away.

"With every mate of mine gone to snipers, shells and shrapnel I felt very lonely among those thousands of men on Gallipoli peninsula. I was the only one left of all the men I'd trained with."

Henry Lewis,
Otago Battalion.

59

The wounded begged not to be left behind. The men were only just kept there by an Australian officer who threatened to shoot anyone who fled. Then New Zealand machine guns opened fire as six shells from the British battleships slammed into the advancing Turks. The hill was covered with smoke and dead bodies. The attack had been stopped and the Turks left alive retreated.

That night Turkish bugles called and war cries of "Allah" grew. Then soldiers were seen on the skyline. They charged all night, desperate to defeat the Anzacs before they became properly entrenched, but they once again ran into the path of hidden machine guns. A New Zealand corporal with a shattered hand handled one machine gun, assisted by several privates. Men fought with their fists and the handles of picks, and between attacks they deepened their trenches before the sun rose. By the dawn of 28 April the attack was over, but the trenches were still too shallow.

Over the next few days soldiers made their way to the cove to rejoin their original battalions. The beach was crowded with supplies, wounded soldiers and men trying to find friends, brothers and fathers. Many men found that most of the soldiers they'd shared a tent with in Egypt had been killed or wounded. Everyone was exhausted — some slept with food in their hands. They were unshaven, uniforms ripped and bloodied and some had camouflaged their hats with branches. Officers had pulled off their badges and pencilled on their ranks so Turkish snipers wouldn't target them. Already a few New Zealanders and Australians were swimming in the sea as shrapnel shells burst high overhead.

The cove looked like a mining camp. The steep hills were covered with waterproof groundsheets and blankets tied to the waist-high scrub and soldiers digging into the banks for protection from

COMMUNICATION: Signallers laid telephone wires to the front-line, where they were connected to portable handsets. Orders were then received by telephone. The wires were repeatedly damaged by shrapnel.

Messages to less secure spots were relayed by runners. So many runners were shot by snipers that orders rarely got through to the front-line in time to be useful.

the hot sun and shrapnel. Back at the trenches, sentries who had barely slept for five days shot or bayoneted soldiers they mistook for Turks. Only the boom of the British battleship guns made them feel safer. Many of the men who died on the first day still lay on the slopes above the trenches. Others were buried overlooking the sea and small white crosses were placed on top of their graves. The area was named Anzac Cove.

WORKING PICK TO MY SHOVEL

In the weeks after the landing, the Anzacs dug trenches and threw sandbags onto the Turkish side to form a parapet. Loopholes were left in the bags so the men could fire through the parapets without showing their faces. The trenches were on the edge of a ridge — there was nowhere to go if they weren't held. The men dug for their lives and soon all they could see was bone-dry clay and the blue sky above.

Some trenches became so deep that 'firing steps' were cut into the walls. Australian Private George Tierney, of the 24th Battalion, knew his brother Arthur was somewhere at Anzac Cove but only found him when he heard him talking in a trench 20 metres away. Men slept on the floor or in 'pozzies' cut into the walls. At night rats ran over them. Maggots that had infested the bodies of dead soldiers pushed through the earth and dropped on their heads. The dust at the bottom of trenches crawled with

"When I got into the trenches at Quinn's I found we were less than twenty yards off the Turk trenches. Between our trenches and theirs were about fifteen or twenty bodies. They were there for the whole time I was in Quinn's Post, about six weeks. The stink was worst at night."

Hartley Palmer,
Canterbury Battalion.

them. The smell of rotting corpses became unbearable. Soldiers tried to incinerate a corpse by spraying it with paraffin and setting it on fire, but the trench just stank of roasted flesh for days.

In safer places, soldiers crawled out into no-man's-land at night, brought the dead back on blankets and buried them in the floors and walls of trenches. Their names were written on pieces of bully beef case.

KEEPING AN EYE ON THE TURKS

Mustafa Kemal ordered snipers to push forward in every possible place. They crept forward, hid in the thick prickly scrub and shot over twenty men a day. In one hour, five Anzacs were shot behind their own front-line. At a place called Suicide Corner, 14 Anzacs were shot in four hours as they tried to rush around the bend. Bridges, the Australian division's commander, was shot in the thigh on the way to his daily tour of the front-line trenches and later died. Men were killed as they carried water up tracks and as they ate breakfast outside their dugouts. The snipers preferred dawn, when the rising sun was behind them, and blinding the Anzacs. The Turkish snipers forced the Anzacs to keep their loopholes stuffed with sandbags so they wouldn't be shot through them. Sandbag barricades were built along tracks and men carrying rations or tins of water would sprint across exposed sections. Watching soldiers would roar with laughter when someone tripped then scrambled to safety.

Unlike the Turks, the Anzacs hadn't been given periscopes and without them they had no idea what the Turks were doing. Many soldiers who looked over the parapets were shot in seconds. They made their own periscopes with mirrors from the ships, cut into small squares and attached to either end of a piece of wood. By the end of May, they had made 3000 and could now watch the Turkish trenches.

QUINN'S POST AND BOMBS

The Anzacs hadn't been given grenades either. When the Turks started throwing their black 'cricket bombs' in late April, the Anzacs knew they'd never be able to win without them. They improvised, making 'jam-tin' bombs on the beach. Empty tins were packed with bullet cartridges, bits of shrapnel, and explosives. Then the lid was tied back on with wire and a fuse attached. In early May, the first two were given to the Australians at Quinn's Post. All the soldiers cheered when they worked. By June, up to 400 bombs were being made a day and bomb-throwing battles raged.

Both sides tried to toss each other's grenades back before they exploded. If they didn't have time, they pulled out the half-burnt fuse or threw sandbags or blankets on top of it, which were blown to pieces, but better that than a person. A few bombs were smacked back with a piece of wood, cricket-style. But many exploded in the trenches before they were thrown back. Hands were blown off, and eyes and faces destroyed.

At Quinn's Post, the Anzac and Turkish trenches were only a biscuit throw apart and they could hear the Turks talking. It was hell, and bomb battles never seemed to end but the soldiers were convinced that if this post fell, Anzac would no longer be safe and getting

A soldier uses an improvised periscope rifle, invented by Australian Lance Corporal William Beech of the 2nd Battalion in May 1915, allowing the Anzacs to fire their rifles without looking over the parapets. (AWM H02310)

supplies to the front-line would be very difficult.

TUNNELLING TO CONSTANTINOPLE

When the Turks started digging tunnels to get under the Anzacs to blow them off the peninsula, the Anzacs responded by digging their own to stop them. The hills became so streaked with dirt that one German observer wondered if he'd wake one day to find the Anzacs had "tunnelled to Constantinople".

The tunnels were just high and wide enough for one man to stand and swing a pick. There were airholes every four or five metres for fresh air, but it was always damp and rank with the smell of a decomposing bodies. When they found a corpse, they'd tunnel around it or drag it out. At night the air-holes were blocked with rags so the Turks couldn't see the candlelight.

A 'cricket bomb' was a grenade about the size of a cricket ball, with a fuse connected to the explosives inside it. The five-second fuse was lit, and then the bomb was thrown.

They dug in shifts, day and night, until they heard the Turks. If they were close enough they detonated explosives against the wall in the hope of collapsing the Turkish tunnel. Otherwise they'd keep digging or wait for the Turks to get closer. Sometimes the Turks were quicker and the explosion would bury men alive.

In late May, Turks from the 14th Regiment exploded a tunnel under Quinn's Post, charged out and captured a section of trench at Quinn's Post. Reserves from the 15th Australian Battalion raced forward, firing their rifles and throwing bombs, forcing some of the Turks into a bomb-proof shelter. The Australians hurled more bombs into the packed shelter killing 23 soldiers. Finally, after the Australians promised they wouldn't kill them, the 17 Turks who were still alive surrendered and emerged into the sunlight where the Australians slapped them on the back and handed them cigarettes.

When the New Zealanders relieved the Australians soon after, parts of the trench were collapsing and sandbags and walls were covered with dried blood. Lieutenant Colonel William Malone, commander of the Wellington Battalion, ordered, "bomb for bomb and bullet for bullet". Any sign of movement from the Turkish trenches was answered with grenade after grenade and sniper teams were sent out in pairs to kill the deadly Turkish snipers. One man watched for Turkish movements, then told the shooter where to fire. Two Australian snipers crawled out into no-man's-land, fired two shots then came back waving a Turk's hat.

"I was in a special detachment of six snipers. We would move round into different positions where we might get a shot at the Turks. You got that good you could shoot the left eye out of a fly."

Sergeant Harvey Johns, Wellington Battalion.

Rumours spread that some of the dead Turkish snipers were found with 20 or more Australian and New Zealand 'meat tickets' in their pockets. One sniper was rumoured to be a woman. Another was painted green and covered with branches, another was dressed in civilian clothes.

It didn't take long for the Anzacs to wrestle control of the firing line back from the Turks. Turkish snipers were killed, their periscopes were shot down, and any sound or movement was met with a shower of jam-tin bombs. Sometimes they were throwing hundreds a day at Quinn's alone. Mules could now be led up the tracks during the day, men sat outside their dugouts without fear of being shot, and loopholes could finally be uncovered. Malone worked his men hard. The trenches at Quinn's were deepened and roofed, chicken wire was erected to stop grenades and shelters were built for the support soldiers to sleep in.

NINE TO FIVE

The soldiers slept in their clothes and boots, with rifles loaded and bayonets fixed. Some men didn't take their boots off for weeks. They worked in rotations: 24 hours in the firing line, 24 hours in the support trenches and 48 hours of 'rest and fatigues'. The men in the firing trenches took turns to watch and sleep. Sentries used kerosene tins for toilets. Whenever a Turkish attack was expected, soldiers would wait in the support trench to replace the wounded or dead in the firing line.

When the soldiers were 'resting' or on fatigue duty, they dug trenches and tunnels, cut roads, and levelled hills to make terraces for water tanks and shelters. At 3 a.m. they

The Anzacs called the ID discs they wore around their necks and wrists 'meat tickets'. When a soldier was killed, his platoon would recover the disc so the next of kin could be identified.

'stood to arms' as this was the time they expected the Turks to attack. The safest time to work was from 4 to 7 a.m. If it wasn't bad enough having to work during the night, the men then found it almost impossible to sleep during the day because of the heat and flies. The men were worked to the bone, to the point where most men preferred being in the firing line as it was nowhere near as exhausting as 'resting'.

LIVING LIKE RABBITS

The men's dugouts were like a second home, decorated with mirrors, photos, flags and pin-ups of women. Some had sandbag walls and were well roofed; others were dug like rabbit burrows, sometimes five to ten feet underground. Australian Private Albert Pickering joked that he was so used to living in his dugout that

LIEUTENANT COLONEL WILLIAM MALONE: Wellington Infantry Battalion Commander. Malone worked his men hard in Egypt, often training them for hours after the other battalions had returned to camp. His men quickly came round to his tough discipline when they got to Gallipoli. He made Quinn's Post a fortress and was more concerned about getting his men home alive than winning the war quickly.

he would "dig a hole in the backyard and live there" when he got home. Others never wanted to come out. One shell-shocked soldier refused to leave his dugout for days and when he was finally coaxed out he was a trembling wreck.

Soldiers read and wrote letters in the light of their smelly 'slush lamp' — a jam or bully beef tin filled with bacon fat with a plaited sack for its wick. The men looked forward to their mail each fortnight even though the letters and newspapers were weeks old. At times writing paper was as rare as water so they wrote on cigarette wrappers, the paper lining of ration cases and even rock-hard biscuits.

THE RULES OF ANZAC

Over time, four rules developed at Anzac Cove. First, toilets were to be used, not bushes. Second, food scraps had to be burnt or buried. Third, no matches or lit cigarettes were allowed in certain places as these drew Turkish fire, and, finally, a soldier's dugout was his home and anyone found in it without a good reason was considered a thief.

BEACHY BILL

Men walked over a mile from the front-line to swim at Anzac Cove and there was an informal competition to become "the brownest man on the beach". No one had bathers so they swam naked. On one day, Charles Bean, Australia's war correspondent, counted over 400 men sunbaking or swimming.

Among them were men from the Indian Transport Corps who had been landed within the first week to transport the Anzacs' supplies on mules from the beach to the front-line. One of the Indians used to sit on the beach, yelling, "Haircut, sixpence." He wasn't the best barber and the mule clippers he used were blunt and painful. When he disappeared one day, rumours spread that he'd been shot as a spy for

The Anzacs believed it was bad luck to light three cigarettes off one match. The flash of the striking match would alert a Turkish sniper. The next cigarette to be lit gave him time to aim and the third was for the shot.

using his mirror to flash positions to the Turks, but it was just as likely shrapnel or a sniper killed him.

The Anzacs cooled down and washed in the sea, but there were few days when shrapnel from Beachy Bill didn't hit someone. Once, shrapnel hit 18 swimmers. Most of the time, the men helped the dying and wounded, then ran straight back into the water. But on days when it was bad, soldiers would run naked from the sea and hide behind the stacks of ration boxes cluttering the beach.

The soldiers nicknamed the deadly Turkish guns. There was Anafarta Kate (or farting Annie) and Lonely Liz, but Beachy Bill was the gun they knew the best.

Most of the men refused to duck when they heard a shrapnel shell explode as they didn't want the Turks to know they were afraid. But whenever they heard a long, slow whistle they knew it was a shell that exploded when it hit the ground and not in the air, metres above them. They'd seen human remains being collected into bags by stretcher-bearers for burial so they ducked when they heard it, certain that their time was up. When they knew they were safe, they'd laugh at others ducking under bushes and blankets or sprinting from the toilet with their pants around their ankles.

Most supplies were landed at night and men would work furiously to unload the boxes before Beachy Bill started up again at sunrise.

Steele's Post, July 1915. (AWM G01076)

Chapter five –
Corpse Flies

What if you were there...
Anzac Cove, June 1915.

This damn dirt. I need a knife to scrape it off my body. The wind whips it up from the trenches and it just covers you and the sweat sticks it to your skin. It doesn't even come off after swimming. If only Mum and Dad could see me like this. Mum would boil all our drinking water for a bath and Dad would just laugh and tell me to clean my act up.

"God, it'd be great to be having a dip back in Napier, Gerald," Reggie says.

"That place is meant to be a hole," I reply, ducking the seawater he splashes at me.

I've never been to Napier but I have to agree with Reggie, any place would be better than here. Most of the time it's like watching grass grow but no matter how bored and tired you get, you're not allowed a second's sleep. I think it's time to get out. It's too hard keeping my head above the water, but Reggie's got a mouth on him and he'd keep talking even if he was 20 000 leagues under the sea.

"You heard that new rhyme the Canterbury boys have made up? I wrote it home a couple of days ago."

"No," I say, sputtering on half the Aegean I just drunk.

"A man don't need a rifle, he hardly ever shoots. He only needs a pair of shorts and a hefty pair of boots. He needs a bloody shovel, to dig the bloody track. And a bloody box of ammo, to hump it, lump it, hump it. To hump it on his back."

"Yeah, I've heard it before."

A shell explodes about the cove and shrapnel slices into the sea. Someone screams and men crowd around and help the wounded man onto shore. That's my cue to get out and me and Reggie make our way in just as another shell explodes not far from where we'd been swimming. That's got us running and we grab our clothes and hide behind a stack of rancid cheese as we get dressed. Once it looks like Beachy Bill isn't going to pay us another visit we head back to Quinn's. We're going into the firing line tonight and I hope that the Turks will charge. All we've been doing for weeks is building shelters, digging and ducking bombs.

"It'd be good to have a go at Johnny, eh Reggie."

He doesn't answer, just grunts with exhaustion. I haven't done anything since I got here except carve my name into the trench walls and shoot that stupid bastard. Not one charge, not one bit of open fighting. But at least I'm on my feet again after crawling to the john every 30 seconds when I was sick. I got a bit weak and there was nothing left in my gut except intestines. It's no bloody wonder I can't brush these damn flies away.

It's a warm calm evening and as we smoke Woodbines we watch the sun sink . These are the moments I enjoy, sitting with friends, more or less not talking and re-reading the last three letters I got from home.

"Sing us a song, Gerald."

I pretend that I don't hear and they don't ask again. They'd probably just want to hear "It's a long way to Tipperary" which I don't care for much. Another hour and it's our turn in the front-line.

It didn't take long for Quinn's to turn to hell but at least it's a bit of fun. We threw a couple of bombs from one of our listening posts at some Turk coughing up a lung. Since then they've been throwing bomb after bomb and they must have exploded against a corpse because the place reeks to high heaven. They're exploding on the roof and shaking the walls and the blasts are lighting up the trench. We're trying to throw as many back but we're not keeping up and it looks like our supplies going to run out soon. Suddenly it's quiet and there's no point working out why they've stopped. I light a fag as the others settle into their pozzies for some shuteye. The battle plays over in my head but this time round the bomb explodes in my hand before I get to throw it. God knows why I imagine these things but it keeps me awake so I play the battle over and over.

Gerald Sievers

STRAIGHTENING THE LINE

On 2 May, Godley ordered the New Zealanders and the 4th Australian Brigade to attack Turkish positions at the Nek. The aim was to close gaps in the Anzac firing line and make one long continuous trench. At this stage Pope's Post was isolated by the rugged terrain and to get to Quinn's Post, the soldiers had to go down to the beach and up another valley. Birdwood, the Anzac commander, had wanted an assault along the whole line but Bridges, the Australian commander, had said his troops were not up to it. Godley should have said the same. He knew there was little chance of success so he planned a night attack to increase his odds. It was the New Zealanders' first chance to prove themselves in attack, and Godley's first time commanding his men in battle. Both would fail to impress. It was raining as Godley told the New Zealanders to "finish them off this time". By the time they left, the slopes were greasy with mud.

They were meant to meet up with the 4th Australian Brigade but the gully they were sent up was crowded with wounded soldiers, which slowed them down. Time was slipping away and they could already hear rifle fire coming from the Nek. The Australians had pushed out on time at 7.15 p.m., but the New Zealanders were only at the top of the gully, pulling themselves by ropes up a slippery slope. Without support, the Australians could do nothing but scratch holes in the ground to hide from the bullets.

It was pitch-black when the New Zealanders got to the top of the rope. Turkish machine guns cut them down before most even had time to catch their breath. They couldn't see anything as they pushed through the scrub. The guns were so loud they couldn't hear themselves speak and the noise echoed around the hills until they had no idea where the Turks were. They hid behind dead bodies, waiting, hoping to be saved. Others cried and prayed to be wounded so the nightmare would end.

During the attack, a New Zealand officer was overheard shouting into a phone for the New Zealanders to "Dig! Dig! Dig! Dig!". But it was too late, they were retreating. The communication was terrible, and Godley, believing his men had gained ground, ordered British reinforcements to support the Australians. They arrived at dawn and didn't stand a chance. The hill was covered with bodies. It was renamed Dead Man's Ridge. As the sun rose the Australian survivors crept back, broken and dirty. One soldier danced on the crest and yelled at the Turks, challenging them to attack. Another cried because he'd lost his bayonet. The men who survived started to question Godley's ability to lead them in battle. The attack was doomed from the start; the Australians had done well but the

New Zealanders had been too tentative and behind schedule. Bean's opinion was that the New Zealander fought with gloves on, whereas the Australian, "when he fights, he fights all in".

HELPING THE BRITISH, 6 MAY 1915

General Hamilton, believing that Cape Helles was the key to victory, decided to launch an all-out attack before the Turks became too entrenched. This time he decided to bring the New Zealand Infantry Brigade and 2nd Australian Brigade to support the British. If they could break through, they could capture the Narrows. The other Australians were left at Anzac Cove to keep Kemal's soldiers away from Cape Helles.

The New Zealand and Australian soldiers landed at Cape Helles on 6 May. The landscape couldn't have been any more different. There were no steep banks to be scaled, only fields covered in flowers, green wheat and dotted with olive trees. Like at Anzac, the screech of a naval bombardment shattered the silence. At the front-line, British and French troops poured out of trenches and

"Would I say we disliked General Godley more than the Turks? I don't know. But he wasn't popular. I certainly didn't like him."

Russell Weir, Wellington Battalion.

charged across open fields in broad daylight. Then Turkish machine guns cut them down. They charged two more times the next day and gained very little ground. Hamilton had wanted a night attack, but Major General Aylmer Hunter-Weston, the overall Cape Helles commander, didn't trust his men because they'd lost most of their officers — he thought they'd start shooting each other in the dark.

In the meantime, the Anzacs marched toward the front. Wounded Lancashire soldiers stumbled back past them as British gun horses and Indian mule carts rushed forward. The Anzacs marvelled at the French soldiers' blue and red uniforms and swapped hat badges and buttons with them and the British. In the morning, a New Zealand and an Australian soldier swapped a tin of apricot jam for two fresh bread rolls and some coffee the French were making nearby. It was a welcome change from their normal tea and biscuits.

A POINTLESS DAY, 8 MAY 1915

The following day, once the sun was up, Hunter-Weston ordered the New Zealanders to seize a hill. That was all he told them — they didn't know their main objective or where the enemy was. They didn't even know there were British troops 800 metres in front of them. Nothing had changed strategically since the failed daylight charges of the last two days.

The New Zealanders ran, under fire, across an open field until they suddenly found the British trench. If Hunter-Weston had sent them under the cover of darkness, they could have made it without losing a man. They slumped next to the Brits and caught their breath, knowing they had further to go. The field in front was covered with red poppies and long-stemmed daises. Strands of fir trees, thick with hidden Turkish machine guns, lined either side. The British soldiers couldn't believe the New Zealanders were going to charge after what the machine guns had done to their men in the last two days of daylight attacks.

THE DAISY PATCH

The first line of New Zealanders charged over the white flowers and the Turkish bullets that missed, ripped earth from the ground like it was hailing. Several men made it to a dry riverbed where they started scraping holes to hide in. Bullets pierced their water bottles and the sun blistered their legs. They could see the Turkish trenches covered with pine logs and dirt, but not one Turk. Other soldiers trying to reach the riverbed were cut to pieces until those that remained refused to charge. By noon the battle was at a standstill.

Hamilton came ashore and saw that little progress had been made. Even though his own officers were telling him that the force was exhausted, he didn't want to admit failure and ordered another attack for 5.30 p.m. This time everyone was included. Brigadier General Francis Johnston, commander of the New Zealand Infantry Brigade, complained that his force would be destroyed if they attempted another day attack, but orders were orders. He then instructed his soldiers to, "Fix bayonets — go right thro — no shilly shally."

The Australians were cooking their dinner at 4.45 p.m. when they were told to march to the front-line. They hurried with heavy packs across flat countryside as a 15-minute naval bombardment shattered the silence. No one knew what they were meant to do. They came to a trench filled with British soldiers and waited there for 5.30.

A piercing whistle blew and wave after wave of New Zealanders charged into Turkish bullets. They zigzagged across the open ground trying not to be hit. Hartley Palmer, of the Canterbury Battalion, decided it was pointless to keep charging after seeing five other men killed in front of him. He dropped to the ground and held his entrenching tool in front of his head. The last line turned back.

The Australians ran almost 1000 metres until there weren't enough men left alive to keep going, then dropped to the ground and started digging. More than one man in three was killed or wounded. The

The disastrous charge of the Australian 2nd Brigade. The dead are strewn across the field. (AWM C01079)

New Zealand Infantry Brigade
2671-strong
771 killed or wounded

Australian 2nd Brigade
2900-strong
1056 killed or wounded

British generals were using their forces as if it was still the 19th century — full frontal assaults across open countryside in broad daylight. The mentality of the British elite who were behind the campaign seemed to be that it didn't matter how many men were sacrificed — Anzacs or British — there were always more. There was no thought of families mourning at home or of soldiers returning without limbs to communities that couldn't understand what they'd been through.

The dead were sprawled over the daisy and poppy fields. The Anzacs knew they'd been sent to their

Hunter-Weston was promoted two weeks later. He left Gallipoli in July, suffering from heat stroke and a nervous breakdown, before being sent to the Western Front.

deaths for no good reason. The Australians turned on Colonel James McCay, commander of the 2nd Brigade, even though he'd just been following orders. The New Zealanders blamed the English commanders. The belief that the Australians and New Zealanders could rely on each other in battle grew stronger. A few days later they were relieved by British soldiers who looked no older than 16. The New Zealanders tried to reassure the frightened soldiers that they'd be safe, knowing full well it was a lie. But life wasn't going to be much better for the Anzacs when they returned to Anzac Cove a few days later.

SLAUGHTER AT ANZAC, 19 MAY 1915

By the end of the first week, half the Anzac force had been wounded or killed and reinforcements were needed. The Australian Light Horse and New Zealand Mounted Rifles arrived at Anzac Cove from Egypt on 12 May, without their horses. As they marched to the front-line the Australian infantry soldiers enjoyed hassling them, telling them they weren't real soldiers and asking where their horses were. An Australian infantry soldier crept out and, pretending to be a Turk, yelled, "Come on you Light Horse. We've heard all about you. We don't mind you as long as they don't send any more Australians." But they were relieved that reinforcements had arrived and that they might finally be given a rest.

Over the next week, a British plane spotted the Turks massing behind their front-line. In the very early morning of 19 May, the Anzacs, knowing a major assault was coming, stood in the firing line, in the reserve trenches and in the gullies and waited. The soldiers were given rum. Bill East, of the Wellington Mounted Rifles, had never touched a drop in his life but swallowed all the drink his sergeant handed him. He passed out, waking only when the battle was over.

Forty thousand voices chanted, "Allah." Then wave after wave of Turkish soldiers charged down the slopes and exploding shells lit the pre-dawn sky. The Anzacs waited until the Turks were almost at their trenches then fired point-blank into them. Rifles became white-hot and jammed and the woodwork of several caught fire. Men's shoulders were black with bruises from the recoil of their rifles. The machine guns never stopped. Soldiers climbed out of trenches and straddled sandbags to get a better aim. Men pleaded to be given a chance to shoot, some even tried to buy a place and in one trench, two Australians fought for a spot. Others hated it. The Turks didn't stand a chance. Private F.H.

Palmer, a Wellington soldier who manned a machine gun, said, "It was murder...the worst moment of my life."

The Turks were only able to get into one Anzac trench. They rushed into Courtney's Post after throwing dozens of grenades, but 21-year-old Private Albert Jacka, of the 14th Battalion, shot and bayoneted most of them and captured two prisoners. He was the first Australian to be awarded the Victoria Cross and went on to become a war hero at the Western Front where he received a military cross. His battalion worshipped him, calling themselves 'Jacka's Mob'.

By the end of the day, trench floors were covered with bullet cartridges and the Turkish attacks were weakening. The Anzacs taunted them as they fled, calling "Imshi yalla!", "eggs-a-cook" and "play yer again next Saturday". Soldiers who stood in the open to shoot the fleeing Turks

The Turkish wounded were piggybacked down the ridge by friends who piled them into carts to be taken along bumpy roads to the Dardanelle coast. Those who didn't die from shock and loss of blood were taken by ship to a hospital in Constantinople, the capital of Turkey. If they recovered and were fit enough, they were sent back to the peninsula, as were the Anzacs.

were caught by Turkish machine guns. Six hundred and twenty eight Anzacs were killed or wounded in the attack.

Birdwood wanted a counterattack, but Major General Harold Walker, the Australians' commander, believed the time had passed. Godley didn't and ordered a charge across the same ground the Turks had just been slaughtered on. His officers refused and one was sent back to Egypt as a punishment. It seemed Godley was prepared to do whatever his superiors wanted, without question. A few weeks later he did the same again. After yet another futile attempt to charge Baby 700, Godley received an order that retreating men should not leave behind equipment. He sent his men back to get the equipment. Thirteen men were killed, 25 wounded. Only a rifle and loophole were recovered.

A CARPET OF DEAD BODIES

Forty-two thousand Turks had attacked all day long on 19 May, and of the 10 000 men hit, 3000 were dead. Over one million bullets had been fired at them. The Turks renamed the hills Bloody Ridge and Red Ridge. The Turkish commanders never tried to attack the Anzac position in that way again.

Before battle, Imams, Muslim religious clerics, would call a prayer and Turkish soldiers would answer, "Inshallah" (May God grant it).

The Australians and New Zealanders watched the wounded lying silently in the sun, occasionally rolling from one side to the other. For many it was the first time they'd ever seen a Turkish soldier up close and for others, it was the first time they'd killed someone. They started calling the Turks 'Johnny Turk' and 'Abdul'. They were 'game fighters' — men who weren't afraid of dying. The Anzacs started respecting them, and realised the Turks were suffering just as much as they were. Men crept out to give the wounded water, and pulled in the dead near the trenches to bury them. At one stage, some New Zealanders couldn't bring themselves to fire their artillery at a number of Turks they could see walking out in the open, because it seemed unfair as they weren't "doing any harm". The Australians at Lone Pine would throw cans of bully beef to a gaunt old Turkish soldier as he collected firewood every morning and he would "salaam" and thank them. Eventually a soldier who was new to Lone Pine shot him. But not everyone at Anzac warmed to the Turks. Lieutenant Hal Young, of the 7th Australian Battalion, kept a tally of how many Turks he shot. He was avenging the death of one of his best mates.

THE TURKS

The Turkish soldiers were fighting for their land and their country. They were defending their country from an enemy — the British, French, Indians, Australians and New Zealanders — who were attempting to invade their homeland. They feared what would happen to their families if they were defeated.

But not all of the soldiers wanted to be at Gallipoli. They weren't all Turkish volunteers; there were also Greek, Armenian, Albanian, and Arab conscripts who didn't want to fight but had no choice. After the 19 May massacre the Turks listened to an Anzac interpreter telling them they'd be well treated if they surrendered. They answered him with bombs and later threw over a note that said, "You think there are no true Turks left. But there are Turks and Turks' sons!"

The Anzacs tried other methods as well. They gave prisoners cigarettes and as much food as they could eat, then sent them out to find firewood. The idea was that they would escape and tell the other Turks how well treated they were but they came back with wood and asked for more food. Other men did everything they could to avoid being captured. One soldier was caught after he got lost bringing water up to the Turks on the back of a donkey from one of the many Turkish wells. He was released with armfuls of food after telling the Anzacs the water was a present from his commander.

ARMISTICE
The bodies of the dead swelled up and turned black

in the heat. The stench was nauseating and green flies flew from the corpses to the men's food. An armistice to bury the dead was arranged for 24 May, from 7.30 a.m. to 4.30 p.m. It was drizzling when the rifle fire stopped on time. The silence was strange. Only tall soldiers were chosen for the burial parties to trick the Turks into thinking that the Anzacs were giants. They met the Turkish burial party in the middle and divided no-man's-land in half with stakes. They weren't allowed to cross the line and were meant to bury their own dead and return the others to the line. But the corpses were so rotten that they couldn't be moved. Instead, the bodies of Australians and New Zealanders and Turks were buried next to each other.

The burial party stuck picks into the swollen bodies to let the gas out. A Turkish doctor gave a New Zealand doctor scented sheep's wool to put in his nostrils to block out the suffocating stench. The dead bodies lay so thick that it was impossible not to stand on them by accident. Ten or more men would dig a shallow grave together, then push 20 bodies in and cover them quickly. The Anzacs buried by the Turks on their side were recorded as missing, believed dead, because their meat tickets couldn't be recovered.

The Turks and Anzacs talked to each other in sign language and an Australian soldier tried to measure the height of the tallest Turk against another Anzac. They smoked each other's cigarettes, swapped biscuits for Turkish bread and pulled buttons from their uniforms in exchange for Turkish coins, as the Turks weren't allowed to remove their buttons.

The soldiers who weren't in the burial parties climbed out of their trenches and stood in the quiet. Others who had never been to the front-line clambered up the hills to the trenches. Just before 4.30 p.m., the burial parties climbed back into their trenches and drank rum and smoked cigarettes to get over what they'd just done. At 4.30 p.m. the silence in no-man's-land was pierced by the noise of thousands of rifles firing and shells exploding. The dead had been buried. The fighting started again.

INFANTRY OF 1915

Army Corps	2 divisions or more commanded by a lieutenant general
Division	3 infantry brigades commanded by a major general
Brigade	4 battalions commanded by a brigadier
Battalion	approximately 1000 men commanded by a lieutenant colonel
Company	4 platoons commanded by a captain or major
Platoon	40–60 men led by a lieutenant

Chapter six —
Waiting for the End

What if you were there...
Anzac Cove, July 1915.

It's a good view, leaning against the dusty bank watching the sun on the sea. The wind's blowing from Australia. I can smell the dead and hear the roosters and dogs in the Turkish villages. My sister's taken the news badly and I sit on her letter so it doesn't blow away. It's the only letter I've got since I've been here but it would've been better if she hadn't written. I don't want to think about home. I only wrote to tell her about Mick being killed and to let Dad know that I was a crack shot, that I'd come third in Egypt in a shooting competition. Corpse flies cover the handle of the bayonet I've driven into the dirt, crawl over my lips and skin. I've given up trying to brush them away. But, in its own way, Gallipoli's a beautiful place.

It's strange that I can't do it. Seems pretty stupid, with the days being so hot and most of the others having cut the legs off their pants. Some men aren't even wearing tops anymore, but I can't do it. I held off in days hotter than this. I still remember how good it felt when I looked in a mirror and saw myself in my uniform. I looked strong, and people, even good-looking ladies, looked at me when I walked down a street. Even my mum seemed to like it.

"What's going on Pete? Have we won the bloody war?"

It's Davo the Ox, soaked with sweat and struggling just to stand let alone carry the two kero tins he's got slung over his shoulder. He's lost weight, looks as skinny as the stick insects you see in museums. I'm meant to be on fatigues as well, but it's too beaut a day to get too carried away.

"Sit down before you stop one."

"Ah, it doesn't hurt much anyways," he says, as the full tins thud to the ground. He slumps next to me and I know I'll be the one who's got to get him to his feet again. Davo got shot through the arm in the first week, then got a couple more holes from Beachy Bill as he made his way back to the beach. The stupid bastard couldn't wait to get back here but I reckon next time he'll do all he can to get home, especially now his brother's gone. We sit there and smoke rollies and I think about nothing. Davo squeezes pus from his leg sores and wipes it on the dirt near my bayonet.

"You finally cutting shorts?"

"Not after seeing your bloody legs."

My pants are torn and threadbare as it is but I don't want to look like Davo when my number's up. I want to be buried in my uniform. I want the others to remember me that way. I rest against the bank and stare at the sky as I take a long drag. It really is a beautiful day.

"Less room for the lice," he says, then adds cheekily, "no one's gonna mind your white pins."

"You heard the latest furphy?"

"What? The one about the English generals asking an Australian private how to win the war."

"Austria's surrendered," I say, laughing at his joke.

It'll be good when the war's over and we can get home but it doesn't seem it'll be happening any day soon. I can't take the flies no more. A couple of shrapnel shells explode close by. I hear a soft thud and look at Davo with his lit fag hanging from his lips.

"You alright?"

He kinda grins and I lie back down and close my eyes and ignore the flies as the sun burns my face. One of the water tins must've been hit 'cos my elbow's wet.

"You've got a hole in one of your tins, Davo. Looks like you'll be making another trip."

He doesn't reply and I know he's dead even though he's still sitting up. He was always talking about how he was gonna buy a tractor for his father with his pay. His hands are clasped like he's praying but he's not religious. I grab the water tins and sweat all the way up to Tasmania Post. I'll come back with the padre and his mates and we'll bury him with the others.

Private Pete Walden

STALEMATE, JUNE TO JULY 1915

On 25 May, a German submarine torpedoed the British battleship *Triumph*. It keeled over, smoke billowing into the sky as other boats tried to rescue the crew and hunt the U-boat. Almost all the fighting in the trenches stopped as the *Triumph* sank. The Anzacs had felt protected by the *Triumph*, so much so that they wanted to be docked a month's pay to have the ship refloated. But the damage had already been done. The rest of the British fleet was removed to the safety of Imbros harbour and was only used when needed. The men felt less protected now.

By June, the Anzacs were bored looking at their clay walls and even the new reinforcements were sick of the war. Most of their battles were now against flies and lice — they could go days without firing a rifle, let alone seeing a Turk. There were no major attacks planned, the weeks of tunnelling were getting nowhere and no one could see an end to the fighting. Most were now sure they'd be at Gallipoli until they died or were wounded badly enough to be sent home. Men took the deaths of friends and others around them in their stride. Few cried — they knew they'd never stop if they started.

The men always tried to make the most of their bad situation. John Skinner, of the Otago Infantry Battalion, used to shoot at a flock of vultures that flew over every morning. He never hit one but it made him happy just to see them change course. The soldiers made friends with tortoises that occasionally slept in their dugouts, searched Turkish bodies for souvenirs and watched the bi-planes fly over. They'd follow each bomb the pilots dropped and cheer as they exploded on the Turkish trenches. But many men feared the long metal darts dropped by the German planes. They were designed to go through a soldier's head down into their body but just about every time they were dropped, they landed on their sides. The men started cheering themselves up by taken out their frustrations on the Turks.

At night they waved flares in front of their bayonets to make the Turks think they were about to attack. Once, some Australians asked them how many would eat a can of bully beef and when the answer came back that many could, they threw a bully beef bomb over and yelled, "Well share that among you." Some of the New Zealanders kept themselves busy painting "Turkish delight, distribution free!" on their artillery shells before firing them at the Turks.

If there was a quiet moment, the men played chess, waved entrenching tools to let the Turks know their bullets had missed, and played poker, gambling with matches. They even arranged a shooting duel between an Australian and Turkish soldier, but a Turk who didn't know about the duel shot the Australian. At Lone Pine, the Australians held up a piece of metal and laid bets on which side a sniper's bullet would hit it. A soldier called 'Bluey' won so many times they started calling him the "luckiest man alive", until the sniper's bullet ricocheted off the metal, killing him.

DRINKING WATER

The soldiers were meant to get four and a half litres of water each day but they were lucky to get a litre, which was used for drinking, cooking and cleaning. When there were problems with the water supply, they'd only get one cup a day. Every morning, the men queued at water tanks to fill bottles and kerosene tins before carrying them back to the trenches. If shrapnel pierced a tin on the way, they had to return for another one. If they were shot, it meant even less water got to the front.

Water was shipped from Egypt then towed from Imbros in water barges. Soldiers who'd been found guilty of small offences pumped it into tanks on the shore. It would then be carted up the valleys on the backs of mules, led by Indian Sikhs from the Indian Transport Corps as shrapnel exploded above, and then transferred to tanks which were guarded by soldiers.

The Indian Sikhs wore turbans and khaki uniforms. They parted their beards down the centre and tied each end behind their ears. If the Anzacs wanted to get along with them, they had to know three rules: human shadows couldn't fall on their food or water while they were eating or they'd throw it away; they'd only take a cigarette from a packet, not from someone's hand; and if they offered food to someone they expected it to be eaten.

SPIC AND SPAN

Each morning the Anzacs collected dew from the waterproof sheets that hung over their dugouts to top up their water ration. After cooking and drinking, the men poured the tiny amount that remained into their tin cups and cleaned themselves with rags. They either shaved their faces with the dregs of their tea or grew beards. When they got the chance, the men washed in the sea, scrubbing their bodies and faces with sand. Some tried brushing their teeth with sea water but most of them stopped after their first try. The hot days were so unbearable that they stopped wearing jackets and shirts and soon cut the legs off their pants — their uniforms were boots, socks and a pair of shorts.

"The living conditions were shocking. Because of the water shortage, tea had to be boiled in dirty pans and it tasted like poison."

Bill Groves, 8th Battalion.

BULLY BEEF AND BISCUITS

The men were allowed three cups of black tea a day. There was sugar but no milk. For breakfast they had bacon, a small piece of cheese, some jam and six biscuits. For lunch, they had a cup of tea. For dinner, they had bully beef and another cup of black tea.

The hard biscuits were like dog biscuits. They were so hard, men broke their teeth on them. Some soldiers just nibbled the edges of the biscuits and chucked what was left into no-man's-land or at the Turks. The bully beef was over-salted, which made the soldiers thirstier, and after being in the heat, the greasy fat would slide across the tin plates.

The cheese was greasy, smelt like the dead in no-man's-land, and the packets often exploded when opened. The men weren't allowed the tins of condensed milk on the beach until they got through all the cheese. From 9 June, an Australian bakery started on Imbros and bread was delivered to Gallipoli every ten days. It was broken into small chunks and divided among the troops but many never saw any, as other soldiers used to raid the rations as

"For dinner we have three courses, water, tea and sugar (lovely). For tea we have bully beef stew (done to perfection).

Sapper Victor Willey, 2nd Field Company Engineers.

they were being taken to the front-line. The fresh beef from Cyprus was often flyblown, left out in the heat for hours and was usually off by the time it was given to the men.

Men stole potatoes and onions when the guards weren't looking. A couple of New Zealanders dug a tunnel through a bank to the back of a ration pile, took what they wanted, then covered the entrance with branches so they could return. Australians used to swap the cases of shrapnel shells with British sailors for bread, condensed milk or tobacco. The sailors sold them to their officers as souvenirs. The Australians sold the bread and milk to other men for profit. Officers always stopped this when they found it happening.

Men returning from hospitals in Egypt or the islands brought back fruit, chocolate and eggs. Sapper Victor Willey, of the 2nd Field Company Engineers, swore that after eating eggs for the first time in weeks, he'd never kill another chicken for as long as he lived. 'Fishing' also became a popular sport. Soldiers

"As for the food, the tins of bully beef stood in the hot sun, in probably 100 or 115 degrees Fahrenheit (46° Celsius) of heat for days and days and days. It was just cat's meat floating around in a tin of oil."

Vic Nicholson, Wellington Battalion.

threw jam-tin bombs off the pier, then dived in and collected the stunned fish floating to the surface. One time, a single bomb brought in a catch of 20 fish. Men also swam out and collected fish killed by Turkish shells exploding in the sea. The Indian's chapatti — similar to a pancake — was a sought-after treat. Because of the lack of vegetables the men were given lime juice four times a day to prevent scurvy. The most generous ration was the tobacco and cigarettes each week, but the dozen matches they were given were never enough to light their cigarettes and fires for a day, let alone a week.

"I was told my share of rice was in the Dixie. I lifted the lid. It was black with flies from the dead men and open latrines. I satisfied my hunger with an army biscuit and a drink of water."

Harold Hinckfuss, Signaller, 26th Battalion.

COOKING RECIPES

The soldiers found ways to spice their meals up. Hard biscuits grated on a piece of tin or smashed in a bag with an entrenching tool made a half-decent porridge when they added water. They minced bully beef with wild thyme collected from the hills, or added water, biscuits and jam to make a stew. For pudding they soaked their biscuits in water with jam. The headquarters staff, Godley, Bridges and Birdwood had cooks making them French toast, omelettes, and meals with fresh meat, tomatoes and lettuce. They even had milk.

Rum was perhaps the most protected item at Anzac Cove. It was given to the men to keep them going. It warmed them in cold weather and helped them dig trenches and roads for a few more hours in the middle of the night. They also drank it before and after battles.

ITCHING ALL OVER

Every time the Anzacs stopped moving their skin crawled with lice. It spread rapidly from soldier to soldier and drove them mad. They'd jump up, wave their arms in the air and scratch their bodies until they couldn't feel them scuttling over their skin. Whenever they could, they'd take off their clothes, turn them inside out and search for the lice. They killed them until their thumbnails were bloodied, then counted how many they got — fewer than 50 wasn't much of a catch. Then they ran a lit cigarette down the seams to kill the eggs. They also tried throwing their clothes into the sea to drown the lice, but the lice clung on.

"FROM THE JAM TO THE CORPSE, AND BACK AGAIN TO THE JAM"

From June to October a plague of flies flew from the

open toilets to corpses, to food. They'd drown in cups of tea and swamp the men's meals. In the first few days the soldiers used the bushes as toilets until deep long drops were dug on slopes exposed to shrapnel. Men sat on a piece of wood supported at either end so they didn't fall in. Their used toilet paper was blown around by the wind. The waste wasn't covered with dirt quickly enough and thick clouds of flies swarmed over it, before crawling into the soldiers' ears, mouths and noses, and over their eyes looking for moisture. Men tried everything — wrapping hessian around their heads, getting friends who'd signed up as reinforcements to bring mosquito netting, and airing blankets over their dugouts' entrances to keep the flies out when they needed to sleep. Every time a bush was knocked a black cloud of flies would rise. They were nicknamed 'corpse flies' and sickness soon spread.

> "You couldn't see the open latrine for flies, flies thicker than anything you'd ever seen. We fought the flies harder than we fought the Turks."
>
> Hartley Palmer, Canterbury Battalion.

A TRIP TO THE TOILET

The 'Gallipoli trots' started in June and was out of control by July. More soldiers were being hospitalised

with dysentery and enteric fever than with wounds.
Incinerators were built to burn empty food tins and mule
manure. The dead were buried but nothing stopped
sickness spreading. The backbreaking monotonous
work, lack of sleep and dysentery were taking their
toll and sick men were collapsing just trying to walk.
Soldiers were passing nothing but blood and the acid
lining of their stomachs.

By July over 200 men a day were being taken from
Anzac to the island hospitals. More should have gone
but only the worst were sent in case the Turks attacked.
The men were given drugs and, so long as they could
stand, were sent back to the front-line. Some soldiers
refused to see the doctor because they didn't want to
be sent away — it would take too long to get back to
Anzac and their comrades.

Men's immune systems collapsed. They became
covered with septic sores after being scratched by the
prickly scrub or cut by tin cans. One soldier had pus
under every fingernail. The hard biscuits had no protein
and the doctors knew that
once men returned to
Anzac from the hospitals,
they'd quickly become ill
again. When the doctors
asked for more medicine,
General Hamilton told

"The truth is, enteric
fever and dysentery
was a bigger enemy
than the Turks."

Russell Weir,
Wellington Battalion.

them to take more care as the Anzacs were using twice as much as the British at Cape Helles. To some, it seemed that Hamilton's staff were far more concerned that Hamilton and his 'top dogs' were well-supplied with soda water than with the welfare of the Anzacs.

By the end of July, just over three months after they'd arrived, the Anzacs looked like scarecrows. Their tattered uniforms hung from their wasted bodies. Their skin was brown and grimy with dirt. Their hair had been shaved short with mule clippers. Anzac Cove was now a graveyard. It was a place of thirst, flies, dust and digging. They were fed up with war. They wanted to go home, but not until they'd finished the job they'd started.

"Doctors didn't excuse them duty. These men just had to keep going. They were so weak some of them just fell into the latrines and died there. They didn't have the energy to duck snipers and didn't care. I saw fellows commit suicide."

Henry Lewis, Otago Battalion.

Chapter seven –
Break-out from Anzac Cove

What if you were there...
Tasmania Post, Anzac Cove, 5 August 1915.
Flies. Their buzzing does my head in more than the smell of the rotting meat they feed on. The trench walls are already shimmering with the day's heat. It's too hot to fart, let alone fight. All I can do is make boot prints in the dust, lick the sweat from my lips and dream of sleep. My back tooth's already giving me trouble and the flies won't shut up. It's gonna be a good day.

Tom, a clerk from Perth, passes me a cuppa.

"Better be sweeter than me, Tom boy," I say, stretching me back and thinking about toast and jam instead of the rock I've got to eat. The tea's black and sweet but I can only chew the biscuit on my good side. I'll have to find some rum and see the dentist when I get a chance.

It's quiet. The Turks are behaving themselves for a change. Tomorrow's our big day. We'll finally break out of this hellhole. I finish the dregs and read the leaves to pass the time.

"What's it say, Pete?"

"Looks like I'm gonna get a holiday wound and end up in London where I'll meet a rich merchant's daughter and never have to work again."

"Here, read mine."

I take his cup. It's not good, but I say, "You'll make it home, but you'll marry a hag and every day you'll wish you were here."

"Not bloody likely," he laughs.

I've lost a few mates since I've been here. Mick's death was the hardest. I still miss him and it cuts me up the way he copped it. I tried but I couldn't take his meat ticket off. His neck was slimy with warm blood and he wasn't laughing or smiling. I couldn't touch him. I wish I could've done it; I owed him that, as a friend. I hope my sis has got over his death. It's a mug's game, this war, but I'll make it home. My tea leaves told me that.

Tasmania Post, 6 August 1915, 5.12 a.m.
Twenty-five of us wait. It's cold and the sun's just coming over the hill we're about to storm. The Turks have been at it since 4.30 a.m., retook part of the trench we got from them a week ago. It's a hell of a racket, shooting, yelling, bombs going off.

"Ready?" a lieutenant calls.

We grab hold of the sandbags above us and wait. The last storming party didn't make it. I don't like our chances but there are men that need our help. I work the rifle's bolt and a bullet slides into the chamber. My bayonet catches the morning sun.

Tom hands me a folded letter. He's as white as a sheet. "I don't think I'm going to make it back, Pete."

I take the letter and say, "I'll give this back after we've cleaned Johnny out." I've never seen him this spooked before. More bombs explode. Someone yells, "GO."

It's always a struggle getting over the parapet and it takes a few yards before I'm running and not stumbling. Tom falls in front of me. Half his head's gone. I fire shot after shot without aiming. I'm in the trench. It's filled with Turks desperate to live. I thrust my bayonet into them, twist and push harder when it jams against bone. I move along the trench, standing on the dead, shooting at Turks further down. Then pain slices into my thigh. I pull the trigger and the wounded Turk lets go. I yank the bayonet out and let my blood run from it onto my hand. A holiday wound. I squat against the trench wall and listen to the cheering. We've retaken the trench.

A couple of mates help me up and slap my back, and say, "You're going to the island hospital, you lucky bastard."

I see Mick's cross as I'm helped down to the beach. It could've been me in his grave and him going home.

Private Pete Walden

LOOKING TO BREAK THE STALEMATE

As far back as May, New Zealand scouts had been creeping up the steep gullies north of Anzac Cove, looking for ways to get behind the Turks. They avoided Turkish outposts and almost got to the summit of Chunuk Bair, one of the heights the Anzacs were meant to seize at the landing. Hamilton and the Anzac commanders decided to take advantage of the lack of Turkish soldiers around Chunuk Bair and made plans to capture the heights and break the deadlock.

Once again the idea was overly ambitious and relied too heavily on surprising the Turks. It wasn't very different from the landing, except the Anzacs were now exhausted and sick with dysentery.

The plan was that once the British at Cape Helles and the 1st Australian Infantry Brigade at Lone Pine had attacked Turkish trenches to draw attention away from the heights, the New Zealanders would seize Chunuk Bair, while the 4th Australian Brigade and the 29th Indian Infantry Brigade would separately assault Hill 971 and Hill Q — two heights above Chunuk Bair. Newly arrived British troops would be held back in support. All this was to be done in ten hours. Once Chunuk Bair had been captured, the New Zealanders would then charge into the back of the Turkish trenches on Baby 700. At the same time, the 3rd Light Horse Brigade would charge across the Nek also to attack Baby 700. Godley was to command the forces attacking the heights. It would be his first chance to prove himself in a major battle after the 2 May debacle. Walker, the British-born commander of the Australian division, was to oversee the Australians at Lone Pine and the Nek.

The soldiers were kept in the dark about the plan, but they knew something was up when they had to prepare Anzac Cove for another 25 000 soldiers. Soon over 6000 British and Indian soldiers were being landed secretly each night. The Anzacs had been waiting for the chance to attack for weeks. They were sure that once they'd broken out of Anzac, they'd defeat the Turks in the open fields and finally march into Constantinople. Either way, it would be better than being trapped in between the sea and 20 000 Turkish soldiers. The number of men at sick parades dropped and soldiers on hospital ships tried to get back. Just about everyone wanted to be with comrades for the final push.

On 5 August, the New Zealanders waited in the sun at Happy Valley. A Maori contingent of 477 soldiers had arrived on 3 July and this was to be their first battle. The New Zealanders sewed white patches on the sleeves and backs of their shirts so they wouldn't mistake each other for Turks. Many were still weak with dysentery. They lay on their backs and thought about the approaching fight. Many of them thought they wouldn't make it back.

AUSTRALIANS, LONE PINE, 6 AUGUST

August 6 was a bloody day from the start. At 4.30 a.m. Turkish soldiers retook Leane's trench which they'd lost a week earlier. The Australian commanders sent two storming parties of 30 men to take it back again. The second party succeeded.

Later that day, the 1st Australian Infantry Brigade also sewed white patches onto their shirts as artillery bombed the scrubby land to destroy barbed wire entanglements. The break-out of Gallipoli had started and the Anzacs could see plumes of smoke from Helles rising into the blue sky. Walker had argued with Birdwood to have tunnels and a secret firing line dug 70 metres in front of the Turkish trenches to increase his men's chance of survival against the fortified Turkish trenches. During the day engineers quietly collapsed the roof of dirt and grass, turning the underground firing line into a trench.

At 4.30 p.m. the Australians took their positions. The front-line filed into the dark narrow tunnels, making their way to the secret firing line, while men in the main trench pulled sandbags down from the parapets to use as a step to get out faster. They waited, smoking cigarette after cigarette. They made sure they were standing next to their mates for the charge. The Turks waited in their underground tunnels for the shelling to end — they weren't expecting an attack. The sun was setting when the whistle screeched three times at 5.30 p.m.

The Australians burst out of the ground right in front of the Turks. The two lines behind scrambled over their parapets and ran forward, tripping on bushes and pieces of barbed wire, before jumping over the secret firing line. The Turkish soldiers not hiding fired their machine guns. Bushes caught fire. Men fell in lines. The Australians found the Turkish trench covered with pine logs and earth. Unseen soldiers fired at them through small holes. They tried to rip up the logs until others found holes big enough to jump into. The trenches were pitch-black and bayonets were thrust until they found flesh. Many of the Turks were taken prisoner before they'd even come out of the tunnels they'd been hiding in. In the uncovered trenches, Turkish soldiers watched for bayonets and shot men as they came around the corners of the trenches. Bodies lay three- or four-deep at some corners. By 6 p.m. Lone Pine was captured. Now all they had to do was keep it — and they knew the Turks would do everything to get it back.

KEEPING LONE PINE

The closest Turkish reserves were a group of exhausted soldiers who'd just been relieved from their trench after 45 gruelling days of being jam-tin bombed. They were just settling down to dinner when they were ordered

After the Lone Pine Battle — Australian and Turkish dead lay on the parapet. (AWM A02025)

to retake Lone Pine. An officer forced the men forward with a whip. They dug firing steps into trench walls with bayonets and fired shot after shot until the Australians were forced back. The Australians threw bombs and shot at the slightest sound as they hastily made posts, piling sandbags across the trenches they'd just captured.

Wounded 25-year-old Captain William McDonald held back the Turks while his men built a barricade. Bombs were tossed to him, with fuses burning. He

> "In the trenches the dead lay so thick that the only respect which could be paid them was to avoid treading on their faces."
>
> Charles Bean

then blew on the fuse before throwing it further. He held back the Turks until the barricade was over a metre high, then stepped behind it. Further back, the wounded flowed through the tight tunnels as ammunition, stretcher parties and reinforcements pushed forward to the fighting. Jars of rum were rushed through to keep the soldiers going.

NEW ZEALANDERS, SEIZING CHUNUK BAIR, 6 AUGUST

As the Australians fought in Lone Pine, the New Zealanders marched as quietly as possible along a widened sap towards the foothills of Chunuk Bair. Sir John Monash's 4th Australian Brigade and the 29th Indian Brigade followed them. By the next morning they planned to have captured Chunuk Bair.

It was now pitch-black. The slender moon was not to rise for hours. For six weeks the British navy had shone a bright searchlight on a covered Turkish outpost and bombed it at 9.30 every night. But tonight was different. The New Zealand Mounted Rifles Brigade and the newly arrived Maori soldiers were there to clear the foothills of Turkish soldiers. Their officers had checked their rifles to make sure they had no bullets in them. The attack had to be as quiet as possible so as not to give the game away for the other brigades. The Auckland Mounted Rifles lay in the dark, just below the searchlight as they waited for the shells to stop falling. Then the searchlight was switched off. The Aucklanders leapt to their feet, scrambled into the trench and stabbed with their bayonets until the trench was taken.

The Aucklanders and the Maoris crept separately up the lower foothills, guessing their way through gullies gutted by erosion and watercourses. They heard rifle fire but had no idea where it was from or if the other groups had been successful. Completely against orders, the deep roar of a Maori haka rang across the hills. It was Te Rauparaha's haka, "Ka mate, ka mate, ka ora, ka

SIR JOHN MONASH: 4th Infantry Brigade's commander. Monash was an excellent military planner but many of the other Gallipoli commanders believed his brigade was undisciplined. He didn't make his name until 1918 when he was one of the first generals to coordinate attacks with the use of air support, artillery and tanks to save lives. He was considered to be one of the best generals on the Western Front.

ora." Trench after trench was rushed. In one narrow trench over 40 Turkish soldiers were bayoneted and in the dark the New Zealanders stood on the bodies and any wounded Turk who moved was bayoneted again. It was an incredible attack — one of the best in the entire campaign. The trenches were stormed secretly in the dark until all the foothills were cleared. But there was a problem — the New Zealanders were two hours behind schedule.

AUSTRALIAN 3RD LIGHT HORSE BRIGADE, TRYING TO CONTROL THE NEK

At Lone Pine, the Australians were still desperately trying to hold the trenches they'd captured five hours earlier. Soldiers of the 3rd Light Horse Brigade — men from Victoria and Western Australia — were keen to prove they could fight just as well as the infantry. They'd been digging and carrying water up steep hills for 11 weeks, but that night they listened to the battle at Lone Pine rage, knowing that the next day would be very different. Many wrote a last letter home.

During the night, turf was pulled down at 21 secret bays close to German Officers — a trench from which Turkish machine guns were trained across the Nek. Birdwood, the Anzac commander, knew that the guns had to be knocked out before anyone charged the Nek — otherwise it would be suicide to attack. At midnight soldiers crowded the dark tunnels but the Turks knew an attack was coming — they watched 21 dark figures scramble out of the bays, then opened fire. Some of the soldiers fell back through the hole. Bodies cluttered the openings and men refused to charge again.

Walker ordered another attack, desperate to give the 3rd Light Horse Brigade every chance possible. Two hours later they clambered out of the bays. The moon was higher and brighter. The attack didn't last long. The Australians had failed — 66 were wounded and 80 were dead. Turkish machine guns still protected the Nek.

NEW ZEALANDERS, SEIZING CHUNUK BAIR, 7 AUGUST

It had taken hours for the New Zealand infantry to make their way up the savage gullies and scrub-covered slopes in the dark. The Otago battalion was shot at all the way and half the Canterbury battalion became lost and returned back to where they'd started. The New Zealanders reached Rhododendron Ridge just after 4 a.m. There was no movement from Chunuk Bair 500 metres above them but they decided to wait for more men. The morning was quiet and the air smelt of thyme. For the first time in three and a half months the New Zealanders were above the Turks and they could see for miles.

4TH AUSTRALIAN BRIGADE, 29TH INDIAN BRIGADE, HILL 971 AND HILL Q

Further north, the 4th Australian Infantry Brigade were lost. They had been led by a local Greek guide along a village short cut so narrow they had to walk in single file. The line stopped and started. Sometimes the men had long enough to sit and, weak with sickness, they fell asleep only to be dragged from their rest when the column started moving again. Then Turkish soldiers who'd fled from the New Zealanders started shooting from the scrub. It seemed like there were Turks behind every bush and the Australians had to fight for every metre. Monash and his men, lost and exhausted, dug in on a ridge far from Hill 971. As they dug, they watched British troops and supplies being landed at Suvla Bay.

During a relatively quiet moment, several Australians crept to an abandoned farm and filled their water bottles with water from a well and robbed beehives of their honey.

The 29th Indian Brigade were also lost and some of the Gurkhas ended up with the New Zealanders.

THE FIRST WAVE, THE NEK, 7 AUGUST

The 3rd Light Horse Brigade's soldiers must have known machine guns were still trained across the Nek as they moved into position. Four lines of 150 men were to charge in waves once the artillery and naval bombardment ended. No more men could fit across the width of the Nek. Two lines of Victorians would go first, followed by two waves of men from Western Australia. The soldiers cut slots for feet and drove pegs into the trench's high wall for handholds. The attack should have been called off. Birdwood knew that the New Zealanders had not yet taken Chunuk Bair and that they wouldn't be attacking Baby 700 but he was determined to draw Turkish attention away from Chunuk Bair for as long as possible.

The men were tired. Four days earlier they'd been pointlessly ordered to hand over their tunics and it had been too cold to sleep. They were to fight in shirts, shorts and boots. It was to be a bayonet charge, no bullets were allowed. At 4.23 a.m. the artillery shells stopped falling. The bombardment had finished seven minutes early. No one knew why. They checked their watches and waited for the shelling to start again.

Turkish soldiers manned their trenches two deep, took aim, and waited. There was no way the Australians were going to make it but they had to try. Other men's lives — the New Zealanders up on Chunuk Bair — depended on their actions. Not wanting to watch all his men die in front of his eyes, Lieutenant Colonel Alexander White, commander of the Victorian 8th

Light Horse Squadron, decided to charge with his men. He shook the hand of the Brigade Major and simply said, "Goodbye."

"Three minutes to go," said White. Then, "Go!" One hundred and fifty Victorians hurled themselves over the top. The quiet was ripped apart by the roar of machine gun and rifle fire. Some soldiers were knocked back into the trenches before they'd even got out. White lay dead. It was over in 30 seconds. Two brothers went over together but only one crawled back. He dropped back into the trench as the second line prepared to charge.

THE SECOND WAVE

It was too noisy to talk. Men shook hands and smiled goodbye. There was no time to think. Two minutes later a whistle screeched and the soldiers scrambled over the top and sprinted towards the Turkish rifles. The bombs they were carrying were hit by bullets and exploded as they ran. For a couple of seconds a yellow and red Australian marker flag was spotted fluttering in the Turkish trench before being pulled down. The few Australians who'd

"The men who were going out were absolutely certain that they were going to be killed, and they expected to be killed right away."

Sergeant Sanderson, 10th Light Horse Squadron

made it, were no longer alive. Out of the 300 who charged, 154 were dead and 80 wounded.

THE THIRD WAVE

At 4.40 a.m. the third line, soldiers from the Western Australian 10th Light Horse Squadron, moved into the firing line. Lieutenant Colonel Noel Brazier, the Western Australian commander, went down to the Brigade headquarters and told the Brigade Major, Colonel John Antill, that the attack should be stopped. But Antill had heard about the red and yellow marker flag being seen in the Turkish trench and he ordered the

"It was like running into a hailstorm and it was not a matter of wondering if I would get hit, but where I would be hit. I saw Colonel White fall — and practically all the rest. I had gone a few yards when I was struck on the hip — it was like a burn. Then a second bullet went through my chest and at the same time another bullet struck me on the right shoulder."

Trooper J.J. Faulker, 8th Light Horse Squadron

charge to continue in support of any soldier who'd made it. The two commanders didn't like each other — Antill thought Brazier was incompetent. If White, the Victorian commander, had not charged with his men, he might have been able to add his weight to Brazier's argument and the third and fourth charges might not have gone over the top. But Antill wouldn't back down. At 4.45 a.m. the Western Australians charged. They probably knew they were going to die. Some decided that all they could do was run as fast as possible toward the Turkish trenches. They dropped like rag dolls.

THE FOURTH WAVE

The fourth line waited in the trench for another 30 minutes. Brazier again tried to stop the charge but Antill refused. This time Brazier went over Antill's head and got permission to attack from another position, but while this was happening another officer demanded to know why the soldiers hadn't yet charged. The men closest to him charged and the others followed their lead. They didn't have a chance.

The bodies of 234 Australians were sprawled in an area about the size of three tennis courts. Turkish soldiers didn't fire at men who crawled to the wounded to drag them in. But many of the wounded who couldn't be reached lay out all day under the hot sun, trying to drink from their water bottles. Down on the beach, soldiers cried when they heard names of friends being read out at roll call. Five hundred and thirty names were called. Only 47 replied and one of those men was being carried past on a stretcher.

Chapter eight –
Everything is Possible

What if you were there...
The Apex, 7 August, 10.05 a.m.
The slope above is covered in bodies and I can smell the rum on his breath as he barks, "You have your orders."

"Well, they're wrong."

"You're to lead your men over and support the others!"

He's a tall, skinny man and I've never liked him much.

"There are none left to support," I snap back.

"They made it to the trench," he demands, his voice breaking like a child's.

"They're all dead, you drunk fool."

"YOU'RE TO DO AS YOU'RE TOLD."

Some of the Aucklanders made it to that trench, I know that, but I'm here to get as many of the Wellington boys home as I can. They shouldn't have been sent in broad daylight anyway. I'm not going to watch my men die because of his incompetence. He grabs my arm when I tell them they're not going to charge but I hold my ground.

"I'll have you shot for disobeying an order."

I can see my men stir and a couple pick up their rifles.
They're good men and I hope every one of them gets home.

"Remember the Daisy patch," I say, knowing that he'd
questioned orders which were suicidal but had still ordered
us to charge. He lets go of my arm and my men relax.
There'll be no mutiny today. "We'll go when it's dark. At
least we'll have a chance of reaching the crest."

It's murder waiting here as we try to hide from the
bullets and shrapnel. Short cries of pain let you know
where the metal's landed. Parsons is taking a sip from
his bottle. He knows better and when he sees me looking,
he screws the lid back on and looks away. He should just
drink the lot because it might be the last drink he'll ever
have. I hope they know that I've done all I can to keep
them alive. I've always refused to send them to their deaths
without a reason, but I remember every one of their faces.
How many more would've died if we hadn't fixed up
Quinn's? I may have worked them hard but it was for
their own good. Tomorrow it probably would've all been
for nothing.

Chunuk Bair, 8 August, 7.30 a.m.
It's only us now. All the men I left in the front trench are
dead and no one can reach us from the Apex. The morning
started off so beautifully quiet but now there's no way
we'll get out of this. Wallace, Jessop and Shoemark and

countless other bodies have been tossed out of the trench and Bruce is holding his guts in and pleading for water. This is our moment of glory, I guess. That's what they'll say. I just hope it's remembered for what it is – a bloody debacle. The Turks are coming at us from everywhere and I can't see them stopping. If only we'd had time to dig in properly. The air reeks of gunpowder.

"How are we going, boys? They'll tire soon, just got to keep going for a bit longer."

Bullets are smacking into the ground all around us and our trenches are nothing more than shallow graves. Gerald Sievers and Gifford are scampering from corpse to corpse stripping them of ammo and water. Someone told me that Sievers was part of the Sistine Chapel choir in Rome and I believe it after hearing him sing.

Here the Turks come again, shooting. I grab my 'rabbit foot' rifle and join the charge. They hate our bayonets so they clear out quick enough. We scurry back to the trench and take cover. I can see Sievers staring blankly back at me, blood running from his nose and mouth. Parsons is near him. More bombs are being thrown and there are fewer and fewer of us. I keep an eye on the crest to wait for the next charge and pray for the night.

Lieutenant Colonel William Malone
Commander, Wellington Battalion

NEW ZEALANDERS, SEIZING CHUNUK BAIR, 7 AUGUST

For some unknown reason, the New Zealanders did not move from Rhododendron Ridge after reaching it at dawn. They had orders to press on but were split up and exhausted. By 6 a.m. the New Zealanders were hidden behind a rise, known as the Apex. It was fully light and any movement from them brought a hail of fire from Turks now dug in behind the crest of Chunuk Bair, 500 metres above them. The New Zealanders had no idea that only 20 soldiers were shooting at them, or that Turkish reinforcements would start arriving at 9 a.m.

In the meantime, the New Zealand commanders argued about what to do. Malone, the Wellington commander, believed it was senseless to attack now that it was light. The Australian charges against the Nek had failed, Monash's 4th Brigade was dug in and the Indian Infantry were nowhere to be seen. He wanted to wait until it was dark. The commander of the New Zealand Infantry Brigade, Brigadier General Johnston, who'd been drinking rum all night, agreed with Malone, but Godley sent orders that they were to continue the attack at once. Turkish reinforcements with 12 machine guns would line the crest of Chunuk Bair well before it was time for the New Zealanders to charge.

An infantryman charging up a ridge at Gallipoli.
(Kippenberger Military Archive, Army Museum Waiouru, NZ)

THE BRITISH SUPPORT

During the night, another 25 000 British troops were landed at Suvla Bay to support the New Zealanders, but again, no one had checked out the terrain. Parts of the bay were too shallow for the barges and men had to wade in water up to their necks to reach the shore. Other boats dropped soldiers off at the wrong place. General Stopford, an ill man with no battle experience, ordered his men to secure the beach before doing anything else. He'd been made a general because of who he knew, not for his ability to command. If he'd ordered his men to advance they could have reached their objectives with minimal casualties — only 1500 Turks were defending the hills — but during the day their snipers picked off hundreds of British soldiers. The British charged several small hills and waited for Stopford to give them new orders but none came. Hamilton should have ordered an immediate advance, but he was 32 kilometres away on Imbros Island.

NEW ZEALANDERS, SEIZING CHUNUK BAIR, 11 A.M.

The commander of the Auckland Battalion kept asking Johnston to wait until it was dark, but Johnston was exhausted and unwell and felt he had to make it up to Godley for delaying earlier. The machine guns hadn't even been set up for a covering fire when he ordered the attack to begin. He cheered on the Aucklanders as they ran over the Apex. Some were so shocked by the intensity of fire that they stopped running until Major Sam Grant, who'd arrived only a month earlier, ran, urging them on. He died from wounds four days later.

The slope was steep and the men had to stop to get their breath back. One hundred metres later they found an empty trench, 46 centimetres deep. The slope behind them was covered with 300 dead and wounded soldiers. Only 111 men had made it and they lay as still as possible, looking back at the Apex to see if anyone else was coming to support them.

The Wellington Battalion had been ordered to go next, but they waited, listening to Malone refusing to let Johnston send them out in the daylight. Malone was threatened with arrest, but he wouldn't budge. His men probably would have shot anyone who tried arresting him. Johnston backed down and Malone's men moved away from the Apex to the relative safety of Rhododendron Ridge. They thanked him. They knew they'd probably die later, but at least he'd won them a chance. But no one was coming to help the Aucklanders now, so they tried to make their trench deeper with the one shovel and two picks they had between them.

For the rest of the day the New Zealanders on Rhododendron Ridge were shot at from the crest of Chunuk Bair. They dug into the hard ground as bullets picked them off. The Canterbury Battalion copped it hardest, losing half their men. A new attack was planned for dawn the next day. Malone told his men to get some sleep but few could. One officer slipped away and shot himself in the knee so he could be taken off Gallipoli. Another lieutenant also took off, but the rest stayed — they had a job to do and they were going to do it. The men's feet were tugged at 3 a.m. They made their way to the Apex as a 45-minute naval bombardment began.

NEW ZEALANDERS, SEIZING CHUNUK BAIR, 8 AUGUST

It was almost dawn when the Wellington Battalion moved from the Apex up a slope so narrow they could only walk 16 across. Then the slope widened and the men fanned out. The New Zealanders back at the Apex watched as Malone's men disappeared over the crest of Chunuk Bair.

Most of the Turks had withdrawn after their leader had been wounded in the bombardment and the few that remained in the trench were quickly taken prisoner except one old man — he was shot reaching for his rifle. For the first time since the landing the New Zealanders saw the all-important Narrows.

One hundred soldiers occupied the trench on Chunuk Bair. It was only a metre deep and they knew they'd be exposed from the waist up when the Turks started attacking but their shovels and picks barely dented the clay ground and each man struggled to fill the two sandbags he'd carried. Malone went with the other 660 New Zealanders to dig a new trench 30 metres below the crest, on the Anzac side.

4TH AUSTRALIAN BRIGADE, HILL 971, 8 AUGUST

Further north, the 4th Australian Brigade marched across fields of recently harvested oats to once again attack Hill 971. Soon all they were doing was digging holes to escape shrapnel and Turkish machine guns. One man would dig while another shot. Then they broke and ran back and many of the wounded were left behind. Private William Watts, of the 14th Battalion, felt as strong as a horse as he ran back, but the second he got to safety, he and every man broke down and could hardly walk. Too exhausted to fight, Monash's Australians would no longer take part.

NEW ZEALANDERS, THE BATTLE TO KEEP CHUNUK BAIR

The Wellington soldiers in the forward trench waited, rifles ready. They knew Turkish soldiers were coming but a slope kept them out of sight until it was almost too late. The Turks attacked from the front and both sides and the New Zealanders, exposed from their waists up, swung their rifles from one side to the other. Wounded men lay in the dirt and reloaded spare rifles for the few men that remained. Some men were firing three rifles, emptying all the bullets of one, before firing the next one, but still the Turks kept coming. Five wounded men tried to

"We got back, and then comes the saddest part of the war — the roll call. All were lined up and names were called. All were friends of someone and there were anxious hearts listening for answers, which in hundreds of cases did not come. It is a horrible thing, this roll call, after a fight."

Private William Watts, 14th Battalion.

get back to Malone's trench but only two made it.

By 6.30 a.m. most of the New Zealanders in the forward trench were dead and soon Private Davis was certain he was the only man left. All the firing on the left had stopped and every soldier to his right was either dead or wounded. He kept firing the three rifles being loaded by a badly injured soldier until they were too hot to hold. He held the Turks back for over half an hour until he was shot. Then Turkish soldiers entered the trench and bayoneted every man they came to, but Davis still had the strength to push the bayonet aside. He kept pushing it away and blood from cuts ran down his arm. A Turkish officer saved him just as the Turkish soldier went to shoot him. He was taken prisoner along with the few other wounded men left alive. Then the Turks charged over the crest towards Malone's trench.

Turkish soldiers and artillery higher up on Hill Q had been firing down at Malone's men since 5 a.m.

"It wasn't long before the dead and wounded were so piled in the trench that we were trampling on them, standing on them, with cover up to our knees. All the time you were thinking, 'What can we do for them?' But there wasn't anything. There wasn't anything you could do for them."

Vic Nicholson, Wellington Battalion.

and it had become impossible to keep digging. Young British troops who'd followed the New Zealanders were cut to pieces. Malone's men were now being attacked from the front and both sides. No one at the Apex could help them. Sixteen men who tried taking two machine guns up were spotted as soon as they left the Apex. Only Dan Curham made it, but he didn't have all the parts for even one machine gun.

The Turks lay behind the crest and hurled bombs, sometimes 50 came over at the same time. The fuses were long so the New Zealanders threw back as many as they could. Just about every soldier threw back at least one or two. Malone urged his men on, telling them it was almost over and that the Turks were tiring. When the Turks crept closer to throw their bombs, Malone grabbed a rifle and led bayonet charges to force them back. His bayonet was bent by a bullet. He kept it for luck.

Men slowly bled to death — bombs fell into

"Men began falling around me. They just dropped, men I'd been living alongside for months, boys from my own town. We had been a close-knit little group, almost brothers. But we couldn't stop or sorrow for the fallen. Our orders were to go on, to the top of Chunuk Bair."

Dan Curham, Wellington Battalion.

There were very few Anzac prisoners of war, as the fighting was so fierce and the wounded were usually killed. Prisoners were treated badly in camps in Istanbul. Turkish prisoners were kept in a wire enclosure on the beach before being shipped to larger P.O.W camps in Egypt.

the trenches and exploded on top of them. Soldiers still fighting wanted to help them but it was hard enough just trying not to stand on them. The day grew hotter and men took off their shirts and fought in singlets or without tops. They collected water bottles and ammunition from the dead. They could see British soldiers swimming at Suvla Bay.

THE VALLEY OF TORMENT

At 9 a.m. the Auckland Mounted Rifles were sent to reinforce Malone. The rifle fire was so intense that they veered off the ridge into a gully where hundreds of wounded men sheltered. Private Burton of the Medical Corps gave his water bottle to an injured Turkish officer who handed it to his five privates without taking a drop for himself. Lieutenant Henderson, an Aucklander, asked about his brother Jack and was relieved to hear that he'd been injured badly enough to be taken off Gallipoli, but Henderson never saw his brother again. He died on Chunuk Bair before the end of the day.

It took three days for the wounded to be carried the one and a half kilometres to the beach by stretcher-bearers. Men died waiting. On the beach, the rows of wounded stretched almost to Anzac Cove. They could see the hospital ships waiting for them, and many, furious at being ignored, called out, "We are being murdered!" Mule-trains carrying ammunition and water for Chunuk raised a fine dust that settled on everything, caking the men's wounds in dirt.

It was after 4 p.m. when the exhausted Aucklanders arrived at Chunuk Bair.

"Soon the ravine was full of wounded. Two hundred of us, maybe more. It was terrible, terrible. We were being shelled too as we lay there. They called it 'the valley of torment'. Men were smashed up, and getting smashed up even more, and bleeding away. They knew they were dying. They were brave men. That's all you can call them. Brave."

Charlie Clark, Wellington Battalion

Malone's trench was so filled with wounded that only the lower parts of men's legs were covered when they stood to fire. An hour later an Anzac shell burst above their trench and Malone, covered in blood, fell back into the arms of another officer. He'd had a feeling he might die and had written home to his wife telling her how much he loved her. His men were devastated by his death. Not long after the sun sank, the Turks stopped attacking and the men, without their tunics or blankets, shivered under the black sky.

THEY DUG ALL NIGHT

The New Zealanders on Chunuk Bair listened to the cries of wounded soldiers all night. Vic Nicholson was sure he heard his best friend Teddy Charles calling out to his mother, then to him for help but there was nothing he could do. It was pitch-black and there were Turks everywhere. Rumours went around that soldiers were shooting the badly wounded to put them out of their misery. At 10.30 p.m. the Otago Battalion and Wellington Mounted Rifles ignored calls for help as they made their way to the summit with food, water, ammunition and bombs to relieve what remained of the British and New Zealand infantry. Out of

"I lost my dearest friend, Teddy Charles, that day. We joined up together and saw the campaign through together until Chunuk Bair...Teddy led thirty men forward to try and hold the ridge. He called, 'come on, Vic,' but I was impeded by Turkish fire. We never saw those thirty men again."

Vic Nicholson, Wellington Battalion.

760 Wellington Battalion soldiers who had attacked, only 70 weren't badly wounded when the unit withdrew. One hundred and seven were dead, 394 were missing, most likely killed.

AUSTRALIANS, LONE PINE, 7 AUGUST

For three more days the Australians and Turks at Lone Pine threw bombs at each other. By the morning of 7 August there were none left and urgent messages requesting more went unanswered. Fifty-four men worked all day making new bombs. By evening all demands from the front were being met.

Turkish reinforcements had to file past a gruesome line of corpses piled four high along either side of the track before fighting the Australians. All night and day they threw 'cricket bombs' around corners and over the tops of the sandbag barricades.

The Australians smothered them or dived around corners if there were too many but the floors still became cluttered with the dead and wounded. Thirty-two trained bomb-throwers of the Victorian 7th battalion rushed to help out. The Australians were desperately holding on.

With no time to bury the dead, the men threw bodies up onto the parapets or dragged them through the tunnels. They wore gas masks to block out the smell. At 4 a.m. on 9 August, the Turks attacked with everything.

Periscope mirrors shattered, bayonets broke in half, and sandbags ripped open. Every spare man shovelled the sand back into new bags. The Turks bombed the Australians out of one post but it was won back. In another post, Corporals Webb and Wright, both from Melbourne, picked Turkish bombs off the ground and threw them back as eight other soldiers

A Greek soldier, fighting with the Turks, surrendered after sticking a white flower into the barrel of his rifle and crawling across no-man's-land.

shot at the charging Turks. Webb had both his hands blown off and died shortly after walking out of Lone Pine; Wright was killed when a grenade burst in his face. Soon there were only two soldiers holding the barricaded post. Then the attack ended — Turkish soldiers were desperately needed at Chunuk Bair to throw the New Zealanders off. The Australians had lost over 2000 men, the Turks 5000. Now all they could do was hope that the New Zealanders could hold Chunuk Bair.

THE LAST HOPE

Seeing his chances of success slipping away, Godley ordered a fresh attack for the morning of 9 August. The Gurkhas and more inexperienced British troops were to take Hill Q. Once again the plan was too ambitious. Godley was meant to attend a meeting at the Apex to discuss the attack but he never turned up, instead he watched the battle from the deck of a destroyer. The now-exhausted Johnston was left to plan it, and against the advice of his staff, he sent the British up an uncharted gully instead of the route the New Zealanders had been using all day. It was a short but steep and unexplored route. They should have followed the New Zealand route, but instead, they became lost in the gully.

The New Zealanders were holding off a furious Turkish attack when the 45-minute British naval and artillery bombardment started in the morning. The Turks were even putting bombs in socks so they could throw them further. The trenches were filled with wounded and the men still fighting lay on the ground and used the dead as sandbags. It was desperate fighting and when a British shell mistakenly exploded among them, some of the New Zealanders panicked and tried to flee. They were held there by other soldiers who threatened to kill them.

The Gurkhas had just driven the Turks off Hill Q after bloody hand-to-hand fighting when the British navy started shelling them too. The Gurkhas, realising they'd been mistaken for Turks, fled. Once again the New Zealanders were on their own. All day long, they listened to a wounded soldier lying in no-man's-land calling out "New Zealand" over and over. There was nothing they could do to help. The Otago Battalion and Wellington Mounted Rifles were going through an ordeal as dreadful as the Wellington Battalion's. At midday, 50 British troops arrived and together they were able to hold back the Turkish soldiers.

At midnight more British troops arrived to replace the New Zealanders, who felt sorry for them — they knew what was coming in the morning. A scout had crawled around the crest during the night and had seen the Turks massing. The British were told to dig for their lives but, once the New Zealanders left, most stopped digging and slept.

CHUNUK BAIR IS LOST FOREVER, 10 AUGUST

In the morning, Mustafa Kemal led his soldiers towards the crest. When he dropped his whip they charged with bayonets and bombs. The British fired as rapidly as possible but the Turks kept coming in waves over the crest and soon they were slaughtered. Further down, British, New Zealand and Indian soldiers panicked and fled as the five lines of Turks charged over the crest. A New Zealand officer fired his revolver at the fleeing solders until they turned back. When hundreds of British soldiers tried to surrender, New Zealand machine guns were fired into their backs. No more men fled but Chunuk Bair was lost. They stayed and fought for their lives and for what was left. Navy shells slammed into the advancing Turks and Chunuk Bair became a "kind of hell". The slopes were covered with Turkish, British, Indian and New Zealand bodies, some knelt with heads in hands, one was still in a firing position. Kemal had thrown just about every man to their deaths and had only just secured Chunuk Bair with his last Turkish reserves. He had no more men left. The New Zealanders held the Apex but they knew they'd failed, and that all their suffering had been pointless.

"If I was asked to give a description of the colour of the earth on Chunuk Bair on the eight or ninth of August, I would say it was a dull or browny-red. And that was blood. Just blood."

Vic Nicholson, Wellington Battalion.

NOTHING LEFT TO GIVE

Walker rewarded the Australian soldiers with seven Victoria Crosses. Only one Victoria Cross was awarded to the New Zealanders throughout the whole campaign — Godley awarded it to Corporal Cyril Bassett, of the New Zealand Divisional Signal Company, for carrying and constantly repairing a telephone wire from the

Apex up to the Chunuk Bair summit under shrapnel fire. Godley never liked praising his men — he didn't believe they should be rewarded for doing what was expected of them. Many of his men believed that dozens of Victoria Crosses should have been given for the Chunuk Bair battle alone.

Out of all the commanding officers, only Stopford would be replaced. Blame was shifted where necessary and most of it fell on Malone for digging a trench in the wrong place. The New Zealand soldiers couldn't believe the rumours that Johnston was being praised for his leadership. Only Walker was prepared to remove useless officers, regardless of who they knew. He also insisted that Australian and not English officers, where possible, should lead Australians.

The Anzacs turned on the untrained British troops at Suvla Bay, blaming them for the failure and deaths of their comrades. The Australians and New Zealanders saw the same qualities in each other and knew they could rely on each other in battle, though others saw differences. From the beginning Birdwood believed that the Australians were strong in attack but weak in defence. The New Zealanders, on the other hand, were considered strong in defence but too cautious in attack. The Australian soldiers were seen as being more Irish — daring and reckless — whereas the New Zealanders were more Scottish — just as daring, but more cautious and prepared to weigh up the costs before leaping into action. It proved true at Chunuk Bair. The New Zealanders missed a valuable opportunity at dawn on 7 August but they made up for it over the next 48 hours, as they held the victory of the whole British campaign in their hands. If they'd been properly supported, Kemal might not have had enough troops left to secure the crest of Chunuk Bair.

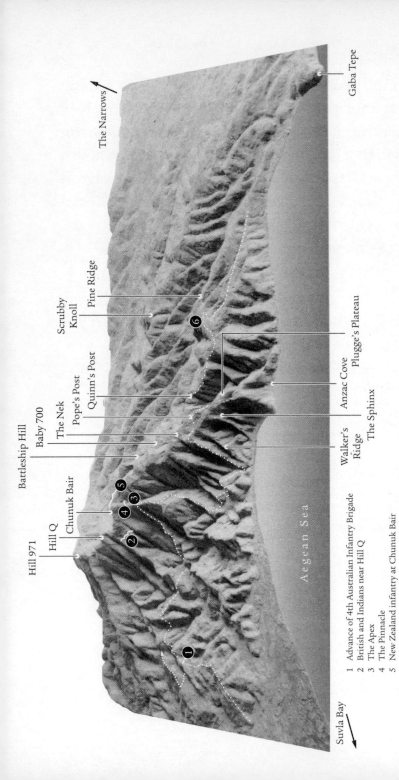

The Narrows

Gaba Tepe

Pine Ridge

Scrubby Knoll

Quinn's Post

Pope's Post

The Nek

Baby 700

Battleship Hill

Chunuk Bair

Hill Q

Hill 971

Plugge's Plateau

Anzac Cove

The Sphinx

Walker's Ridge

Aegean Sea

Suvla Bay

1 Advance of 4th Australian Infantry Brigade
2 British and Indians near Hill Q
3 The Apex
4 The Pinnacle
5 New Zealand infantry at Chunuk Bair
6 Lone Pine

The established line after the August offensive is shown thus: ....

Chapter nine —
Defending Home

What if you were there...
Bloody Ridge, September 1915.

Reinforcements — if you can call 15-year-old boys that
— have arrived. They jump up every half hour to try and
see the English, but they will soon learn. The rest of us are
fed up with this war, but the new kids think this place is
a game. Wait until they're holding a dead friend in their
arms — then they'll stop looking. I puff my lieutenant's
water pipe and wait for the English to teach them a lesson.
They are good at that. One of the boys has a smile like
Adem. He'll be ten now and out in the fields harvesting
with his mother. This war better be over before he's 15 or
else all this would've been for nothing. The kids are getting
braver than a tomcat, daring each other to keep their heads
in the open longer. The Australians must be sleeping.

"Sit down!" I roar. The last thing I want is jam bombs
disturbing my pipe and coffee. They see the Australian
hat on my head and I can tell they know who I am. Umit
the murderer. I've killed some men and they think I'm a
hero but I'm nothing more than a coward. I've been here

three months too long and all I want is for this war to end. Inshallah.

I've only charged the enemy once and I never want to do it again. That is when I lost everyone I knew and I've been alone since. There is no one here to sing our songs or talk about Sariz with. I only talk to the lieutenant because of his pipe and the better food he's got. He's an ass and if he didn't have the parents he's got he would've never been allowed in the army let alone been made an officer. The morning we charged, the Imam spoke to us and filled me with courage. We all nodded when he told us that Allah would be with us. I was sure that we'd win and I'd finally get to go home. Many times since then I've thought about just walking back to Sariz but how long would it take for the English to be burning down my house? I will stay and fight here.

There were 12 of us from Sariz and we made sure we were next to each other when the time came to charge. We scrambled out of the trench and my heart sank when I saw the ground covered in bodies. If I'd been on my own, I would've turned back but my friends were next to me and we ran together. We jumped and tripped over bodies and the English, they let us come close and I thought we might get into their trenches but they were always watching us down the end of their rifles. Then they opened fire and we dropped like trees to the ground. I said my friends' names out loud as each one fell. I wanted to kill the English then, *more than I ever had before or since. I wanted to thrust my bayonet into them but a bullet hit me and I was knocked over. I lay there not moving, surrounded by bodies with tangled limbs. I watched the English shooting and I couldn't do a thing. The sun was unmercifully hot and the buzzing of flies got louder and louder and my shoulder ached and throbbed as the day dragged. I could see Hasad but I could not reach him. I spoke his name quietly but he didn't hear me. When the rifles stopped, the land was covered with death and the dying called to their fathers and mothers. I crawled back to our trenches that night and the men were quiet but very angry.*

I've killed 39 English soldiers since then but that's not enough and I will keep hunting them. I'm a good shot and I'll kill the 120 before I go home. Only then will Hasad and the others be avenged. Then I can return to Sariz.

Umit Bey
2nd Battalion, 47th Regiment,
16th Turkish Division

BEHIND THE TURKISH LINES

After months at war, very few of the Turks wanted to surrender, but many wanted to return to their families. Flies pestered them just as much as they did the Anzacs, and illness spread through the army. Like the Anzacs, the Turkish soldiers were either too proud to leave or the doctors wouldn't send them to hospital as they needed as many men at the front as possible. To stay alive they worked on their trenches, covering some of them with timber and iron salvaged from the bombed villages nearby. The trenches became so dark that they hung kerosene lanterns just to be able to see what they were doing. At some places wire was strung over the tops to prevent jam-tin bombs rolling in.

It made Mehmed Fasih, a 2nd Lieutenant at Lone Pine, feel like "a bird in a cage". Mehmed had only been out of military academy for one year when his division was sent to Gallipoli to defend Lone Pine. He was badly wounded in May and sent to a hospital in Istanbul. In October he returned to fight the Anzacs.

Most of the Turkish trenches were kept uncovered so they could charge. When jam-tin bombs landed, the soldiers would try desperately to pull out the fuse or throw them back. Mehmed hated how much noise his men made when their friends were wounded; he knew the 'enemy' would target more bombs at the commotion. In one attack, two grenades killed two men and seriously wounded four. But the Turks never gave up. They threw thousands of cricket bombs and learnt to shorten the fuses so they'd explode before the Anzacs had time to throw them back. Sometimes they put them in socks and linen bags so they could throw them further, and so the Anzacs wouldn't be able to find the burning fuses in the dark.

When artillery shells exploded in the trenches, Turkish stretcher-bearers had to collect what remained of the dead for burial. Then soldiers in the support trench would move into the firing line and stand where men had been killed minutes earlier, knowing they'd probably die next. Those who couldn't read the Koran, prayed.

In the middle of the night, they would crawl out into no-man's-land to drag back their dead. Sometimes the trench floors and parapets became their graves, but they also buried their dead in cemeteries in the valleys behind the trenches. Mehmed got permission to bury his dead sergeant in the officers' cemetery. The sergeant's friends laid olive and laurel branches across his chest as Mehmed read aloud the first verse of the Koran.

PASSING TIME

At night the soldiers sang folk songs and talked about when the war would end. The songs were always the same but the singers from the beginning of the war had been buried and replaced by new men. There always seemed to be a shortage of uniforms. Many of the Turks wore a mixture of summer and winter uniforms, and some had no shoes. They crept out at night and stripped clothes and boots from dead Anzacs.

Like the Anzacs, the Turks used to play games to pass the time. One time a soldier waved a spade in the air and yelled, "better luck next time" after a sniper's bullet missed him. They started throwing notes and messages into the Anzac trenches, telling them to cheer up because they'd soon lose the war and be back home, free from Gallipoli. They also threw notes promising to treat the Anzacs well if they surrendered. One afternoon a tin periscope was raised and it was immediately shot at so a Christian cross, made from tin, was raised to see if the Anzacs would shoot at the symbol of their religion. They didn't have to wait long.

The Anzacs played their own games. Australian soldiers at Lone Pine used to taunt Mehmed. Once they kept him awake all night by yelling, "we are coming" at intervals. He was convinced that they only threw bombs when they were bored — everything would be quiet and peaceful then suddenly a couple would come hurtling over.

The Turks heard the Anzacs yelling "bastard" so often they wondered if it was one of their gods.

Once some New Zealanders filled a jam tin with pig bones, fat and explosives and threw it into the Turkish trenches, hoping to offend the Turks' religious beliefs by covering them in pork.

WAITING FOR THE END

At the end of August the Turks observed the Muslim festival of Ramadan. They didn't eat anything during the daytime and celebrated its end with a three-day feast. The Anzacs had been warned that the Turks would launch a 'fanatical attack' to coincide with the festival but the soldiers threw cigarettes, raisins and sweets to the Anzacs, who threw cans of bully beef back. The Turks attached notes saying, "Take with pleasure, to our heroic enemy." They asked for condensed milk and when yet another can of bully beef was chucked over instead, someone threw back a note wrapped around a stone, which said, "Bully beef, non!"

Most soldiers lived on olives, dates, dried figs and bread. They'd return to mess tents in the valleys to get their rations. In the morning they ate a bowl of gruel and in the late afternoon they'd have soup, which, if they were lucky, might have pieces of meat in it. For some of the soldiers who'd served in the Balkan War two years earlier, it was better than the grass they'd eaten then. As an officer, Mehmed drank black coffee, ate cheese, sausages and hazelnuts and smoked his water pipe. The lower-ranked soldiers washed their clothes in cauldrons beside a stream, while officers, like Mehmed, washed in bathing tents back at base camp in a valley behind the trenches. Inside, large underground ovens heated the air.

With no reinforcements left, and it looking like the war would never end, Mehmed's men were becoming tired and fed up. They'd lost the will to attack and no longer even shot at Australian periscopes. Instead they crept out at night and stretched barbed wire in front of their trenches. Those that didn't volunteer for patrols were publicly humiliated into taking part when their officers demanded to know what their father and their village would think of them.

Many of the soldiers were peasant farmers who'd never left their local region before and very few could write home to their families. Some thought they were fighting Greeks, not the Anzacs. Older men from the villages visited Gallipoli with spoken messages from their area. They passed them on to sons, fathers, or brothers, before taking answers back to their families. Even though they were still in their homeland, most of the soldiers were homesick. One soldier deserted and walked home. Other men shot themselves so they'd be sent to hospital, even though they knew they'd be executed if they were found out. But most men, even if they wanted the war to be over, kept fighting.

THE ENEMY DISAPPEARS

For three days in November there was no sound or movement from the Anzac trenches. Turkish soldiers stood above their parapets but were not shot at. Mehmed saw that the Australian loopholes were closed. He wrote in his diary, "nothing moves there". Very few bombs were thrown. When the Australians at Lone Pine did throw jam tins, the Turks scrambled for cover, then realised they actually were filled with apricot jam. If the Australians were laughing, the Turks didn't hear them.

Turkish soldiers threw notes into the Anzac trenches asking if they were in good health and to please reply. They took advantage of the silence by creeping out into no-man's-land and shooting at the Anzacs from new hiding places. They decorated their friends' graves and gathered firewood out in the open.

Hooks were cast out into no-man's-land on the end of ropes to catch and pull down the Anzacs' barbed wire. One hook became snagged so firmly that the rope had to be tied around the waist of the strongest soldier to pull in. He soon realised that the hook wasn't caught on a tree root but was being pulled in the other direction by the Australians. Other Turks grabbed the rope to help their friend and soon it became a tug of war. Suddenly the rope snapped, the men fell backwards into a heap, laughing.

Eventually Turkish officers sent out patrols to see what the Anzacs were doing. They were ordered to bring back proof they'd reached the Anzac trenches. Patrols heard the Anzacs talking in whispers, and a rumour spread that a Turkish patrol had brought back a periscope rifle as proof. Mehmed's patrol returned empty-handed, so he ordered them to bring back an Australian loophole as proof that they'd investigated. The patrol heard noises and threw grenades. The Australians shot them.

After three days things returned to normal and the Turks decided that the Anzacs must have been preparing for winter. The weather was turning cold. Mehmed gave the sentries socks and gloves to keep warm. It got harder to find wood and the trenches became muddy and slippery. Mehmed wondered how he'd be able to charge the Australians in his boots — he couldn't even walk down his trench without sliding most of the way.

Chapter ten —
Coming Home

What if you were there...
Wairarapa, October 1915.

There's a knock at the door and my heart sinks. No one knocks during the day. I wish I'd asked my friend Helen what I really wanted to know. How is she coping? Her eldest killed in some place called Krithia and her only other child sitting in the shadowy corner without a hand and half his face gone. I made sure that I looked at him as he drank his home brew and asked me how the farm was going. He didn't say a thing about what it was like there but at least he said Gerald was doing okay and that his songs cheered them up. I wanted to ask more about Gerald, but I don't think he wanted to talk about it so Helen and I chatted about when we could next get to Wellington and have Devonshire tea at Bingles teahouse.

There is another knock at the door. It was such a childish conversation. I wished I hadn't had it.

He stands on the porch, water dripping from his coat and hat. It's still raining hard. He's young, no older than 17 and his hands are red with cold and his face wet and glum. Every hour of every day I've dreaded this boy and this knock on our door.

"Good afternoon. Are you Mrs. Sievers?"

He passes me the cable and I smile but my hand is trembling. This must be a mistake. He turns to leave.

"The fire's lit. Would you like to warm your hands?"

"Thanks Ma'am, but there's more homes I've got to get to."

"Of course."

He rides off and he soon disappears into the rain. The wind is icy cold and I should go back inside but I can't believe I've lost my boy. He was so young and naïve. I want to hold him. I can't go back inside.

I go to find Tom and soon my socks are muddy and wet through. My dress is heavy with water and it drags over the grass and sheep droppings. We should have let him go to Rome. He had such a lovely voice and he paid for all those lessons. He was over the moon when they accepted him but we wouldn't let him go. It wasn't the proper thing for a man to do.

I can see Tom across in the open shed making sure the lambs are suckling. This is a miserable piece of land and I know I'll hate it forever. No wonder he read so many books. He'd read them until he fell asleep and I don't know how many times I had to tell him off after the candle almost set fire to his bedpost. The last time it happened he said to me, "Okay Mum, I'll only read the Bible from now on." I knew he was lying but it was the loveliest thing he could have said.

Tom's seen me in my socks and without a coat and he rushes out to me. He knows. I hand him the telegraph as he wraps his coat around my shoulders. He can't look at me. He knows.

"Tell me he's wounded, Tom. Please."

He opens the cable and the ink starts to smudge. Tom's reading it but I can't hear his words. I can read Gerald's name and "missing in action, believed dead". How can he be missing? How? Tom's tears are being washed away by the rain and he's using all his strength to hold me up. It's my noises I can hear and I know I'll never stop feeling like this. I can't stand the thought that people are going to read his name in the paper.

"I don't want visitors, Tom. I don't want to see anyone."

He's pulled me up and is hugging me tightly. He knows how I feel. He walks me under the shelter of the shed and I can smell the oil of sheep. Nothing will be the same again.

Mary Sievers
Wairarapa, New Zealand.

THE FINAL MONTHS

After the August failures, the Anzacs felt like old men. They'd given all they could but Hamilton wanted more. They were sent to take a hill between Anzac Cove and Suvla Bay but there were barely enough men to walk, let alone charge the Turkish trenches. The New Zealand Mounted Rifles could only muster 300 out of 2000 men, the 4th Australian Brigade only had 500 fit soldiers. It was to be another day attack even though their officers had requested a night attack. On Hill 60 scrub caught fire and the soldiers, some fighting only in boots and shorts, could only watch as flames covered the wounded and dead, exploding their bombs and ammunition. The Turks shot anyone who tried to crawl from the fire. After a week of fighting, the Anzacs captured parts of the hill but the Turks were still above them.

Men now wanted a rest; they'd done enough and many had lost the will to keep fighting. The sick list grew. Soldiers no longer tried to stay at Anzac if they were ill. Soldiers were ducking and hiding from innocent noises and some were happy to receive minor wounds — a 'holiday wound' was a ticket off the peninsula. When the wounded were loaded onto barges, other soldiers watched them with envy. It wasn't just the Anzacs who felt this way — Turkish soldiers were raising their hands above the trenches, holding them up until they were shot.

In September, Australian reinforcements arrived and the worn-out soldiers were sent to rest camps on Imbros and Mudros islands where they ate fresh meat and vegetables. They had their first hot wash in months and bought over-priced grapes, tobacco and alcohol. The days were sunny and the men found the quiet strange. But Anzac haunted them. They could see the faint haze of Gallipoli and they knew they'd soon be returning there. New Zealand reinforcements arrived one night to find the camp as silent as a ghost town. Tea had been made for them but only one man met them — everyone else lay quietly in their tents. No one wanted to talk about Gallipoli.

It wasn't long before they were ferried back, even though the doctors considered them unfit to continue. Some soldiers were glad they were going 'home', but others dreaded it. Maybe this time there would be a bullet marked with their number. Anzac had changed. There were massive tents, a Y.M.C.A and a post office erected on the land they'd won in August. The trenches on Rhododendron Ridge had been improved and now had dugouts in their sides.

Gallipoli was now a stalemate. There were no more frontal assaults, just scouting and patrols. Everyone was digging deeper homes into the clay banks, barbed wire was strewn across the slopes and the days were growing colder. The flies died off. There was less chance of the Anzacs being shot as most tracks were either out of sight of Turkish snipers or protected by walls of sandbags.

BACK IN THE HOME COUNTRY

The soldiers' families had no idea about the conditions the men were living and dying in. Articles written by journalists who visited the peninsula were heavily censored — even soldiers letters to parents and siblings were censored, with words and whole sentences crossed out. Any fears the public had were only confirmed by reading the growing list of casualties in the paper. It wasn't until late September that the truth about Gallipoli was leaked.

Ellis Ashmead-Bartlett, an English journalist, was certain that there would be a major disaster if the British and Anzacs were still on the peninsula when winter arrived. Keith Murdoch, an Australian journalist, offered to take an uncensored letter to London for Ashmead-Bartlett but he was arrested and the letter confiscated. Murdoch then wrote

"At the present time the army is incapable of a further offensive. The splendid Colonial Corps has been almost wiped out."

Ashmead-Bartlett's confiscated letter

his own letter to the Australian Prime Minister, based on what he could remember from Ashmead-Bartlett's letter. It was a mixture of fact and exaggerated errors, but it stressed that the campaign was doomed to fail, especially with General Hamilton as its commander. The letter was published in British newspapers and soon the British Government started talking about evacuation.

JUST STAYING ALIVE

A small storm lashed the peninsula, smashing piers and washing the water-barges onto the shore. Ashmead-Bartlett's predictions were coming true. It would be impossible to supply the forces once winter set in. The Serbian capital, Belgrade, had also been captured by the Austrians. Soon Germany could send troops and heavy artillery directly to Turkey by train and then to the Gallipoli Peninsula. At the end of October, Hamilton was recalled to London after the campaign failures and because he refused to consider an evacuation. General Monro — who believed that all troops and guns should be at the Western front — visited the peninsula and was shocked by the situation. He watched the weak Anzacs struggle up banks to defend the tiny amount of land they'd won. There were no places for rest and the food and water supply depended on good weather. He didn't have to stay long to make up his mind.

"The Staff seem to have carefully searched for the most difficult points and then threw away thousands of lives in trying to take them by frontal attacks."

Ashmead-Bartlett's letter

The Anzacs didn't know that an evacuation was being considered. They were preparing for winter and the men now lived on rumours and hopes. They wanted to blow up mines under Turkish trenches or wash them out of the trenches using a high-powered hose, but, either way, they didn't have enough men to attack.

Lord Kitchener, Britain's Secretary of State for War, arrived in early November and walked along the front-line. Indian troops knelt as he passed and the Anzacs ran for their cameras. It was a quick visit, but enough for him to make up his mind. He ordered an evacuation, though he expected over 50 per cent of the men to be wounded or killed. The soldiers were not to be told until the very end. For the remainder of November plans were secretly drawn up for the evacuation of Anzac and Suvla Bay — the British troops at Cape Helles would remain as there weren't enough boats to take everyone off at once. All surplus men and animals were to be taken off over eight days until there were only 20 000 soldiers left. These troops would then be removed over two nights.

THE SILENT BATTLE, 24 NOVEMBER

Towards the end of November, the Anzacs disappeared. All work stopped, no one walked along visible roads, and there was no shooting or bomb throwing unless absolutely necessary. The 'silent stunt' had begun. The Anzacs wanted the Turks to get used to long periods of silence so they wouldn't become suspicious during the evacuation. When the Turks began investigating, the Australians and New Zealanders let them get as close to their trenches as possible before firing. The Turks seemed to believe that the Anzacs just wanted some peace and quiet as they prepared for winter. The Anzacs enjoyed the quiet so much they extended the silence for another 24 hours.

THE BLIZZARD, 27 NOVEMBER

On the last night of the silent stunt, heavy rain fell, then snow. Trenches became running streams and the centimetres-thick layer of dust in most dugouts became mud. Then a freezing gale blew down from the Black Sea. Some sentries were found frozen to death, still standing with rifles in their hands. Soldiers rushed to the supply depots and got as many clothes as possible — greatcoats, tunics, two pairs of singlets, two pairs of socks and balaclavas.

Icicles hung from the parapets. Wet trenchcoats froze — one stood upright on its own for two days until it thawed. The New Zealanders were given whale fat to rub into their feet to prevent frostbite. The men boiled ice and snow after the water in the tanks and their water bottles froze.

The Anzacs were lucky that only one trench at Anzac filled with water. At Suvla Bay, the heavy rain rushed down the valleys, carrying dead Turks and mules, and flooded the British soldiers' dugouts and trenches. Men were trapped and drowned. British and Turkish soldiers had to get out of their trenches and light fires in full view of one another. Over 15 000 troops, 11 000 from Suvla alone, were taken off Gallipoli suffering from exposure and frostbite.

No new water or supplies could be landed and the Anzacs were put on half rations; half a cup of water, two hard biscuits and rum to warm them up after each shift in the firing line. They wondered how they'd survive a whole winter on the peninsula.

RUMOURS OF EVACUATION

Heavy German shells started falling at the beginning of December, burying men alive. The Anzacs quickly started digging deeper and bigger dugouts to escape the German bombs, as well as the approaching winter. Some were so big that concerts were held in them. New Zealander Alexander Aitken played the violin he and his platoon had smuggled from New Zealand to Gallipoli

— a broken E-string had been replaced with telephone wire. Food and clothing were given out so freely that the men had to dig new shelves in their dugouts. They'd been starved for months, but now they ate like generals on tinned chicken, roast pheasant and soup made from tablets. Rumours started spreading about an evacuation.

From 10 December, mule trains silently snaked along roads at night, carting concealed artillery to the piers. Officers were told to thin their ranks in preparation for winter and more and more companies were removed to the islands. Any soldier who complained of the slightest illness was immediately taken off Gallipoli. Most thought they'd be returning, but on 16 December, they found out the evacuation rumour was true.

LEAVING OLD FRIENDS BEHIND

The men were torn. They were relieved to be finally leaving Anzac but few wanted to quit what they'd started, especially after so many had died — what would the dead think of them, and those back in Australia and New Zealand? Some wanted to charge one more time rather than run away. They had all dreamed about leaving Gallipoli, but not like this.

At night, they crept out to visit the dead in no-man's-land for the last time. They visited the small cemeteries, tidied up graves and erected new crosses. They hoped the dead wouldn't hear them leaving. British planes flew over the front-line all day to prevent German planes spotting the lack of troops. Smoke from Turkish fires loomed above them. The foul smell of the wet earth reminded Australian Sergeant Edwards of a graveyard.

Most of the mules, horses and guns were removed. Ammunition was buried or dropped at sea. Tins of condensed milk were punctured with bayonets. All the stone jars of rum were smashed with hammers; they couldn't risk a drunk soldier giving their plans away. Not that it stopped some soldiers, who got down on all fours and lapped up the rum until creosote, a cleaning product, was added to the flow. Picks and shovels were dropped down dry wells and all stores that could be burnt were piled into stacks and doused with kerosene and petrol. One stack accidentally caught fire in the night and the flames lit up the whole cove. The Anzac's luck held — the Turks didn't see the lines of men waiting to be loaded onto boats.

By the morning of 18 December, only 20 000 men manned the trenches. Half of these would start leaving in three stages from midnight. The Turks had noticed the ships coming in and out of the cove but, thinking it was preparations for a Christmas day attack, had just put out more barbed wire. To make sure the Turks didn't suspect anything, men walked the remaining mules up the valleys, played cricket and lit thousands of campfires so the smoke could be seen all over Anzac.

It was dark when the first groups of men walked down tracks marked with salt and flour so they could find their way. Their boots were wrapped in socks and sandbags to muffle any noise. Torn-up blankets had been placed on trench floors, hard earth broken up and all the wooden piers were covered with sacks. Groups of ten soldiers, married men first, walked onto the piers and boarded the boats. Time seemed to drag forever before the boats pulled away from the beach. Up in the hills, the remaining men lit slush lamps in the empty dugouts. By morning only 10 000 soldiers remained.

The Anzacs prepared their trenches and dugouts for the Turks: some left deadly booby traps while others left letters, praising them for being brave fighters and hoping they'd meet again in better circumstances. In one spot, meals were placed on tables and a phonograph with a record called "Turkish patrol" waiting to be played. Hundreds of horses and mules were shot. A soldier who'd ridden his horse most days along the beaches was devastated to find it dead. The remaining New Zealanders tossed coins in the air and called, "Heads for Constantinople; tails for Cairo." After midnight the final withdrawal started.

All along the firing line the first groups of soldiers left the trenches and moved down the tracks to the beaches.

Fifteen minutes later, the second groups followed. It had been timed perfectly and for a change everything ran like clockwork. An officer stopped one group of New Zealanders because they were two minutes early. Men found it difficult not to run the second they turned their backs to the Turks. By 3 a.m. there were only 1500 men holding a line of ten kilometres. They were the 'last ditchers', the 'diehards', soldiers picked for fitness and skill, who were to stay behind and hold back a Turkish attack while the others got on boats. Men had rushed to volunteer and those not picked complained to their

Soldiers playing cricket on 17 December 1915 to distract the Turks from the evacuation. Shells were passing overhead throughout the game. (AWM G01289)

officers, saying they'd been there from the beginning and had a right to be there at the end. Trenches that had been crammed with men for eight months were now eerily empty. The Anzac trenches were soon to be held only by the dead.

DIEHARDS

Each diehard had grenades, a rifle and bayonet. They stood ten metres apart, boots wrapped in sandbags, shooting out of loopholes at the night sky and tossing grenades every half hour. The 1500 men had to convince the Turks that there were still 40 000 men holding the line. They smoked packet after packet of cigarettes so the strong smell of tobacco would add to the illusion. They could see the barges taking the men out to the boats and wondered if the Turks could also see them. Behind them, barricades of barbed wire were in position, ready to be dropped across communication trenches and gullies if the Turks discovered the evacuation and attacked. At the same time battleships would bombard the valleys and trenches. They knew they'd all die if the Turks attacked and the 15 minutes they waited before leaving seemed like it would never end.

After that time was up, the diehards left the firing trench for the last time. On the Apex, one of the last New Zealanders leaving could hear the Turks erecting more barbed wire. Men solemnly walked past the places where friends had died. It was dark and cold. They had lost — it had all been for nothing. A massive Anzac mine under the Turkish trenches at the Nek was detonated and the Turks opened fire, charging forward to occupy the crater and stumbled into the Anzac trenches in the dark. A bullet hit Australian soldier Raymond Bennett — he was the only soldier to die in the evacuation. Private Pollack had been sleeping in a dugout during the evacuation and woke to find the trenches empty. He raced down to the beach terrified that he'd been

A delayed action device for firing a rifle, by means of weights operated through water escaping from one tin into another. A rifle could be left to operate up to 20 minutes after the device was set. Rifles were scattered across Anzac Cove as the last soldiers left. (AWM G01291)

left behind. He was just in time to get on one of the last boats. A British naval officer called out into the dark to make sure no one had been left behind, then the last boat steamed away from Anzac. It was the best-planned action of the whole eight-month campaign. If as much preparation had gone into the landing or August offensive, the campaign could have been very different.

British battleships shelled the petrol-soaked stores left on Anzac Cove. The soldiers on the transports drank hot cocoa and devoured steaming pea soup as they looked at

On the night of 19 December, Mehmed Fasih looked at the crescent moon and saw a halo of seven colours around it. His friend told him it was a sign of a miracle and a good omen. At 3.30 a.m. Mehmed woke and noticed that the front-lines were unusually quiet. There were no grenades. It was the last morning of the Anzac evacuation. A few minutes later he was told, "the enemy has withdrawn".

Anzac, lit up by the massive fires, for the last time. When the sun came up, Turkish soldiers walked through the Anzac trenches and took the pencil-marked crosses from the Anzac graves and burnt them for warmth. On the Greek islands the Australians were each given a

Five Turkish officers watch the Allied ships withdrawing. (AWM A05297)

cooking billy as a Christmas present. It had a picture of a kangaroo knocking a Turkish soldier off the Gallipoli Peninsula with its tail. Written under it were the words, "This bit of the world belongs to me."

On 8 January, the British at Cape Helles were attacked by the Turks, but their lines of defence were so strong that, for the first time, the Turkish soldiers refused to charge. The next day, the British and French evacuated Cape Helles, three weeks after the Anzac evacuation.

After eight months of fighting, over 86 000 Turks were dead, another 184 000 wounded. Over 21 000 British, 1594 Indian, and nearly 10 000 French soldiers died. The Anzac toll was 8709 Australians killed and 18 500 wounded and 2721 New Zealand dead and 4752 wounded.

THE FORGOTTEN ANZACS

Before Gallipoli, the Anzacs had looked up to the British. Nine months later they knew they were not only equal to but better than the British Regulars. A pride in their country had grown. The Australians and New Zealanders were honoured to be called 'White Gurkhas' by the Indian soldiers. The Anzac spirit was growing. The men, against all odds, had proven themselves as New Zealanders and Australians. They had stood by their mates and stuck to their jobs.

Back in Egypt, the Anzac Corps was split up and the New Zealand Division and the Australian Divisions went as separate forces to France, where they would encounter hardships worse than Gallipoli. They would charge across open ground, fight beside tanks for the first time, and walk over fields so muddy that when horses fell off the duckboards, they disappeared under the mud. They were gassed, and lived and died in

"You wonder whether it's worthwhile or not fighting for freedom. There's no freedom when nobody's got a say in anything."

Bill East,
Wellington Battalion

New Zealand, like Britain, introduced conscription in 1916. Australia did not, and were proud they remained a volunteer force.

trenches for another three years. The New Zealanders were nicknamed 'the silent division' as they rarely sang or boasted about their deeds. They kept to themselves and tried to avoid any distinction. Very few of the Anzacs went on from the failed Gallipoli campaign to the Western Front. Many never recovered from illness and wounds and were shipped home. The men wanted to forget about Gallipoli — it was not something they were proud of. They'd left dead comrades behind and the land they'd won — land they considered theirs — had been given back to the Turks. There were still some good memories: the mates who laughed with them and helped them through, swimming on sweltering hot days, collapsing in the shade of their dugout.

On 31 October 1918, the Ottoman Empire surrendered unconditionally. Germany surrendered on 11 November 1918 — the war was finally over. Later, Australian and New Zealand soldiers went to Gallipoli and stood on the hills they had never been able to capture. They would return home to a nation of people who had little idea what they had been through, and had to cope with what they'd seen and done on their own.

REMEMBERING ANZAC

On 25 April 1916, one year after the Anzac troops landed at Gallipoli, the two nations commemorated the first Anzac Day. By the late 1920s, Anzac Day was a public holiday and law protected the word 'Anzac' — no business was allowed to use it for commercial reasons. There was even a proposal to change the Tasman Sea to Anzac Sea.

For the men who'd served in the First World War, Anzac Day became a day to get together and have a drink with old comrades. Every day of the year they thought about the friends they'd lost. The bleached bones of their friends had been collected from the slopes of Gallipoli and buried in cemeteries cared for by the Turkish government. Plaques and memorials recorded the names of those who died without a proper burial.

The Australians and New Zealanders went to Gallipoli as subjects of the British Empire — Australian and New Zealand citizenship didn't exist until 1949. What they went through there was described in newspaper articles as a "baptism of fire". The Anzac legend was born the moment the men set foot on the shores of Gallipoli. Australia has used the experience of Gallipoli, and the myths that have grown up around it, to help define an independent national identity — even to the point of excluding New Zealand. Politicians and newspapers rarely mention New Zealand soldiers around Anzac Day — seeming to forget what the 'nz' in Anzac stands for. New Zealanders, in contrast, have tended to forget or downplay their own role at Gallipoli.

The myths of Anzac help us to remember the bravery and mateship of the soldiers, but they also oversimplify the hardships and fears they endured, and Gallipoli's terrible legacy. As Dan Curham said, "I have felt their loss very deeply for the rest of my life, right to the present day. Talking about Gallipoli, especially about Chunuk Bair, brings sorrow to my heart even as I talk to you now."

Ninety years on, Anzac Day is a chance for Australians and New Zealanders to commemorate all the wars we have been in, even if little is said about the reasons politicians sent young men to fight or why these men volunteered — many had gone for the adventure of a lifetime.

None of the Gallipoli Anzacs are still living (though Australian and New Zealand soldiers went on to fight together under the Anzac banner on occasions in the Second World War, Vietnam and Timor) but Anzac Day celebrations have been steadily swelling in size in Australia and New Zealand. It has become popular for backpacking Australians and New Zealanders to flock to the Gallipoli peninsula for Anzac Day. We now understand Anzac to mean not just a location or a past Army Corps, but a spirit that we believe defines and separates us from other nations. But to have a real understanding of what Gallipoli means, we need to look beyond the myths. We need to try and imagine the lives of the men who fought there and those who never came home.

Those heroes that shed their blood and lost their lives, you are now in the soil of a friendly country. Therefore rest in peace. There is no difference between the Johnnies and the Mehmets to us, where they lie side by side in this country of ours. You, the mothers, who sent their sons from far away countries, wipe away your tears; your sons are now lying in our bosom and are at peace. After having lost their lives on this land they have become our sons as well.

Atatürk — Mustafa Kemal

TIMELINE

1914

28 June	Archduke Ferdinand assassinated.
28 July	Austria declares war on Serbia.
3 August	Germany, declares war on Russia, invades Belgium.
4 August	Britain declares war on Germany.
15 September	First day trenches dug on Western Front.
15 October	Ten New Zealand transports leave Wellington for Australia.
29 October	Turkish (German) Battlecruisers bombard Russian ports.
1 November	Australian and New Zealand transports leave Australia for Britain.
2–5 November	Russia, Britain and France declare war on Turkey.
3 December	Australian and New Zealand transports arrive in Egypt.
25 December	Unofficial Christmas truce on Western Front.

1915

1 February	4th Australian Division arrive in Egypt.
2 February	Turkish army attacks Suez Canal.
19 February	British Navy attacks Turkish forts.
17 March	General Hamilton arrives to plan invasion.
18 March	Last ditch naval effort to destroy forts.
29 March	Hamilton inspects Anzac troops.

9 April	Bulk of Anzac force leave Egypt for Lemnos Island.
25 April	Anzacs and British forces land on Gallipoli.
8 May	Anzacs attack Turkish positions at Cape Helles.
12 May	Australian Light Horse, New Zealand Mounted Rifles arrive at Anzac Cove.
19 May	42 000 Turkish soldiers charge the Anzac lines.
24 May	Armistice to bury the dead.
6 August	Campaign begins to seize the peninsula heights. Australians charge Lone Pine.
7 August	3rd Light Horse Brigade charges the Nek.
8 August	New Zealanders capture Chunuk Bair.
10 August	Chunuk Bair lost.
17 October	Hamilton recalled.
13 November	Lord Kitchener visits Gallipoli.
24 November	The 'silent stunt' begins.
27 November	The 'silent stunt' ends, the blizzard begins.
16 December	Troops informed about evacuation.
19 December	Last night of evacuation.

1916

9 January	Last British forces evacuate from Cape Helles.

1918

31 October	Turkey surrenders.
11 November	First World War ends.

Glossary

Artillery: Heavy guns able to fire long distances.

Bob: Slang for old Australian and New Zealand currency.

Bootblacks: Young Egyptian shoe polishers.

Brigade: A formation of several battalions.

Cakewalk: An easy task — something that can be easily accomplished.

Cruiser: A large, fast warship; smaller than a battleship.

Dixie: An army cooking pot.

Duckboards: Wooden planking placed over muddy areas.

Enlisting: Joining the army, navy or airforce.

Firing steps: A step for men to stand on in order to fire over the parapet.

First World War: From 28 July 1914 to 11 November 1918, conducted mainly in Europe and the Middle East between the Triple Entente (Great Britain, France and Russia, supported by other countries including Australia and New Zealand) and the Central Powers (Germany and Austria-Hungary, aided by Turkey and Bulgaria).

Furphy: A rumour.

Gurkha: Famous Hindu soldier from Nepal, renowned for their fighting skills.

Gallipoli trots: Diarrhoea.

Gyppo: Nickname the Anzacs called the Egyptians.

Haka: Traditional Maori war dance.

Hippies: Scooped-out hollows in the sand for the men's hips to make sleeping more comfortable.

Hun: Nickname for a German soldier.

Infantry: Soldiers that fight on foot with bayonets, rifles, machine guns and grenades.

Johnny: Nickname for Turkish soldiers.

Maorilander: New Zealand nickname.

Meat ticket: Nickname given to the identification discs the Anzacs wore.

No-man's-land: Unsecured area between opposing armies.

Pacifist: A person who opposes violence and war.

Parapet: A low wall of sandbags thrown in front of a trench to protect soldiers from enemy fire.

Pozzies: Nickname of holes in the trench walls that the men used to sleep in.

Recruitment booths: Booths or stalls where men enlisted in the army.

Redcaps: Military Police.

Revolver: A type of pistol.

Salaam: A deep bow — a Muslim expression of goodwill.

Sap: A deep narrow trench.

Stalemate: Where neither side can make any progress.

Sultan: The ruler of the former Ottoman Empire.

Tommy: Nickname for a British Regular Soldier.

Typhoid/Enteric fever: an infectious disease spread through dirty water and food that causes red spots, high temperature, weakness, stomach pain, and possibly death.

Victoria Cross: Highest medal awarded for bravery in the British Empire.

Wazza: Area of Cairo filled with pubs and brothels.

Western Front: Line of battle in Western Europe where the French and British fought the Germans.

Woodbines: A popular cigarette in 1915.

Acknowledgments

Scarecrow Army would not have been possible without the earlier, hard work of many other historians and writers. I am particularly indebted to Charles Bean, Christopher Pugsley, Maurice Shadbolt and Florence Breed. Thanks to the Australian War Memorial for checking the manuscript. Big thanks to my editor Alison Arnold for making it possible, and to Clare Moleta, for pulling me out of the trenches of writing and back to reality.

Select Bibliography

Aitken, Alexander, *Gallipoli to the Somme: Recollections of a New Zealand Infantryman*, Oxford University Press, 1963.

Akçelik, Rahmi (ed), *Before and after Gallipoli. A Collection of Australian and Turkish Writings*, Australian-Turkish Friendship Society publications, Melbourne, 1986.

"Anzac", *On the Anzac Trail: Being Extracts from the Diary of a New Zealand Sapper*, London: William Heinemann, 1916.

Askin, Mustafa, *Gallipoli: A Turning Point,* Turkey, 2003.

Bean, C.W., *Official History of Australia in the War 1914–17, Vols. 1 & 2*, Angus & Robertson Ltd, 1921, 1924.

Boyack, Nicholas and Tolerton, Jane, *In the Shadow of War: New Zealand Soldiers Talk about World War One and Their Lives*, Penguin, NZ, 1990.

Breed, Florence (ed), *From Gallipoli with Love. Letters from Anzacs of the Wimmera — 1915*, Donald, Vic, History and Natural History Group of the M.L.A. Society, 1993.

Cavill, Pte H.W., *Imperishable Anzacs. A Story of the Famous First Brigade*, William Brooks & Co. Ltd. 1916.

Diggers Stories: Memoirs of the A.I.F. by a Returned Soldier, Sydney: Rockwell Printing, 1918.

Fasih, Mehmed, *Lone Pine (Bloody Ridge) Diary of Lt. Mehmed Fasih*, Denizler Kitabevi, 2001.

Fewster, Keven & Basarin, Vecihi & Basarin, Hatice Hürmüz, *A Turkish view of Gallipoli Çanakkale*, Richmond, Vic., Australia : Hodja, 1985.

Fowler, J.E. (Chook), *Looking Backward,* Roebuck Society Publication, 1979.

Gammage, Bill, *The Broken Year*, Penguin Books, 1990.

Hinckfuss, Harold, *Memories of a Signaller. The First World War 1914–1919*, 1982

Knight, F.F., *These Things Happened: Unrecorded History, 1895–1946*, Hawthorn Press, Melbourne, Australia, 1975.

Malthus, Cecil, *Anzac: A Retrospect,* Whitcombe and Tombs Limited, New Zealand, 1965.

Moleta, Christine, *To Music,* Æolian Press.

Pugsley, Christopher, *Gallipoli. The New Zealand story,* Reed Publishing, New Zealand, 1998.

Shadbolt, Maurice, *Voices of Gallipoli*, Hodder and Stoughton, 1988.

Acknowledgments

Treloar, J.L., *An Anzac Diary*, Alan Treloar, Armidale, NSW, 1993.
Waite, Major Fred, *The New Zealanders at Gallipoli*, Whitcombe and Tombs
    Limited, 1921.

Websites
www.ku.edu/carrie/texts/world_war_I/Mons/mons2.htm
www.kultur.gov.tr/portal/tarih_en.asp?belgeno=5303
www.gallipoli.gov.au
www.awm.gov.au
www.firstworldwar.com

Quotations
Introduction
"If I had not stopped this," quoted in
    Bean, Vol. II, page 733
Chapter one
"Australia will stand," quoted in Bean,
    Vol. I, page 16
"If there is to be war," quoted in Bean,
    Vol. I, page 16
"In the evening," quoted in Hinckfuss,
    page 3
Chapter two
"Who are you," quoted in Waite, page
    29
Chapter three
"We were given orders," quoted in
    Breed, page 272
"I am not ordering you to attack,"
    quoted in Akçelik, page 54
"It's as hot as hell up there," quoted in
    Cavill, page 75
"Dig, dig, dig," quoted in Bean,
    Vol. 1, page 461
Chapter four
"With every mate," quoted in Shadbolt,
    page 25

"When I got into the trenches," quoted
    in Shadbolt, page 32
"Bomb for bomb and bullet for bullet,"
    quoted in Pugsley, page 288
"I was in a special detachment," quoted
    in Shadbolt, page 54
"Dig a hole in the backyard," quoted in
    Breed, page 232
Chapter five
"A man don't need a rifle," quoted in
    Malthus, page 90
"Finish them off this time," quoted in
    Pugsley, page 177
"Dig! Dig! Dig! Dig!" quoted in
    Pugsley, page 184
"When he fights, he fights all-in,"
    quoted in Pugsley, page 171
"Would I say we disliked General,"
    quoted in Shadbolt, page 40
"Fix bayonets — go right thro," quoted
    in Pugsley, page 199
"Come on you Light Horse," quoted in
    Treloar, page 153
"It was murder," quoted in Pugsley,
    page 220

"You think there are no true," quoted in Bean, Vol. II, page 162

Chapter six

"Well share that," quoted in Gammage, page 108

"The living conditions were shocking," quoted in Breed, page 272

"For dinner we have three courses," quoted in Breed, page 207

"As for the food," quoted in Shadbolt, page 91

"I was told my share of rice," quoted in Hinckfuss, page 12

"From the jam," quoted in Waite, page 165

"You couldn't see the open latrine," quoted in Shadbolt, page 32

"The truth is," quoted in Shadbolt, page 60

"Doctors didn't excuse them duty," quoted in Shadbolt, page 27

Chapter seven

"In the trenches the dead," quoted in Bean, Vol. II, page 532

"Three minutes to go," quoted in Bean, Vol. 2, page 613

"The men who were going out," quoted in Bean, Vol II, page 619

"It was like running into a," quoted in Breed, page 176

Chapter eight

"We got back, and then comes," quoted in Breed, page 181

"It wasn't long before," quoted in Shadbolt, page 94

"Men began falling around me," quoted in Shadbolt, page 47

"We are being murdered," quoted in www.ku.edu/carrie/texts/world_war_I/Mons/mons2.htm

"Soon the ravine," quoted in Shadbolt, page 66

"I lost my dearest friend," quoted in Shadbolt, page 93

"If I was asked to give a," quoted in Shadbolt, page 94

Chapter nine

"A bird in a cage," quoted in Fasih, page 115

"Better luck next time," quoted in Askin, page 29

"We are coming," quoted in Fasih, page 50

"Take with pleasure," and "Bully beef, non!" quoted in Bean, Vol. 2, page 822

Chapter ten

"At the present time," and "The staff seem to have," quoted in http://www.gallipoli.gov.au/1landing/letter.html

"Heads for Constantinople," quoted in Waite, page 285

"This bit of the world," quoted in Breed, page 277

"You wonder whether it's worthwhile," quoted in Shadbolt, page 79

"I have felt their loss very deeply," quoted in Shadbolt, page 49

Index